GIRL
DO HONOURS

G000138148

GIRLS DON'T DO HONOURS

Irish Women in Education
in the 19th and 20th Centuries

edited by **MARY CULLEN**

◇

Women's Education Bureau

Each essay © the author, 1987
This collection © WEB, 1987

Girls Don't Do Honours: Irish women in education in the 19th & 20th centuries.
1. Women — Education — Ireland — History — 19th century
2. Women — Education — Ireland — History — 20th century
I. Cullen, Mary
376'.9415   LC2072

ISBN 0 905223 97 7 (Pbk)

The Contributors

Tony Fahey is a sociologist by profession. He is currently director of the Development Education Support Centre in St. Patrick's College, Drumcondra, Dublin.

Anne V. O'Connor teaches in Alexandra College, Dublin.

Eibhlin Breathnach teaches in St. Louis High School, Rathmines, Dublin.

Grainne O'Flynn is an education and research officer with the Teacher's Union of Ireland.

Damian Hannan is a research professor at the Economic and Social Research Institute, Dublin.

Richard Breen is a senior research officer at the Economic and Social Research Institute, Dublin.

Maria Slowey lectures in Recurrent Education at Newcastle-on-Tyne Polytechnic, England.

Mary Cullen lectures in Modern History at St. Patrick's College, Maynooth, and is a co-director of the Women's Studies Unit, Irish Foundation for Human Development, Dublin.

Typeset and Printed by Argus Press,
Malpas St., Dublin 8.
Cover Design: Deirdre Cullen.
Distribution: George Philip Services Arndale Road, Wick, Littlehampton, West Sussex BN17 7EN, England.

Contents

Introduction

Mary Cullen

Education has always been a primary concern for feminists. Each of the seven contributions in this book focuses on a different facet of women's educational experience in Ireland. Three — those by Tony Fahey, Anne O'Connor and Eibhlín Breathnach — deal with the nineteenth century and three — those by Gráinne O'Flynn, Damian Hannan and Richard Breen, and Maria Slowey — with the second half of this century, while my own contribution is largely theoretical. Several of the essays summarise and reflect on findings of major research, most of which is not otherwise readily available to the general reader. The range over two centuries and the variety of issues examined provide a context for cross-reference and comparison over time.

One of the most powerful impressions to emerge from the book as a whole is that of the strength and persistence of sex-role stereotyping in moulding the educational experience of women. The studies by Anne O'Connor and Eibhlín Breathnach show feminists in nineteenth-century Ireland breaking through limitations imposed on the education of girls and women. These limitations might be summarised as a list of four explicit and two implicit regulations:

— You shall not study as wide a range of subjects as males.
— Where you do study the same subjects you shall not study them to the same intellectual level.
— You shall not enter the universities or the professions to which they provide an entry.
— You shall study a limited range of academic subjects and cultural subjects to accomplishment level only as well as domestic skills necessary for your future.
— To sum up, you must not have an education that might encourage you to develop your intellectual powers fully or might equip you to compete with males for economic, social or political power.
— Finally (and this underlies all the others) you must not have an education that would stimulate you to challenge the patriarcha stereotypes that control your life and encourage you to take personal responsibility for deciding your own destiny.

1

The discriminatory educational system was only one part of the overall patriarchal organisation of Irish society. Irish society, in turn, formed one unit in the patriarchy of European society as a whole. Women were excluded from participation in political decision-making by election or appointment to office or by voting for the election of men. Property and inheritance systems channelled economic resources and power into male hands and away from female. The universities and professions were closed to women. The law made women the punishable party in sex-related offences such as adultery, prostitution and illegitimate birth. Marriage and domestic life were seen as women's proper sphere but within that sphere the law gave the husband complete authority over the children, the wife and the wife's property.

Ambivalent or contradictory aspects of some of the roles played by women in the education of women emerge in relation to nuns in these two studies and in Tony Fahey's essay. Fahey looks at the exponential growth of the career of nun as a respectable alternative to marriage for middle-class Irishwomen in the nineteenth century. He places this new career in the historical context of the changing role prescribed for female religious by the church establishment. This involved a complete reversal of the previous position as the emphasis switched from the containment of dangerous female sexuality to active, and viturally asexual, participation in the church's new mission to win the allegiance of the proletarian masses in a newly pluralist Europe. He finds that the nuns' primary purpose of religious formation in practice admirably served the state's primary purpose of inculcating obedience to constituted authority. Their success in the latter area is attested to by the golden opinions they won from the national school inspectorate. Fahey also raises the perennially fascinating question whether the nineteenth-century career of nun inhibited or contributed to the development of feminist awareness among Catholic women.

O'Connor's and Breathnach's studies, both looking at the same period, find nuns at second and third level helping in the implementation of the feminist revolutions in education. These revolutions broke through the limitations imposed on the education of girls and women. They also involved the provision of secondary school curricula which prepared girls for competition in public examinations and of colleges to educate women for university degrees. In each case the barriers protecting male monopoly were first breached by a small group of Protestant feminists. But Catholic women followed swiftly once the openings were provided, and the nuns responded to pressure from the Catholic middle-class by providing the required teaching. At second level this examination-oriented curriculum had to find some form of accommodation with the French convent tradition then sweeping Ireland with its emphasis on religious formation, ladylike accomplishment rather than intellectual formation, and preparation for marriage and domesticity. At third level both Protestant and Catholic women had to actually provide new institutions and here again the nuns, Dominicans and Loreto in particular, responded to the pressure and provided colleges which prepared young women for degrees.

The research of both O'Connor and Breathnach show nuns to have been capable of insisting on the new departures in the face of episcopal disapproval. They also indicate that the driving force behind the new departures came from the Catholic middle-class families. Their work and that of Fahey raise a host of questions to be answered about social, economic and attitudinal change in Irish society; about nuns' perceptions of themselves and their role; about decision-making within middle-class families; about the development of feminist awareness and the development of a political and social environment which permitted, if it did not encourage, its expression.

The studies by Maria Slowey and Damian Hannan and Richard Breen examine aspects of women's education in the later decades of the twentieth century and Gráinne O'Flynn's personal reflections are centred on the middle of this century. By this time feminists had succeeded in dismantling most of the overt restrictions on women's autonomy and activity. Few legal discriminations remained. All levels of education and all areas of knowledge were now formally open to both sexes. Yet the pattern and the concerns remain amazingly similar. Feminists are disturbed about 'boys' subjects' and 'girls' subjects' and about the disproportionate numbers of women who pursue studies to the highest levels — and particularly in areas of knowledge seen as 'masculine'. Women have entered big business, the professions and the market-place but are congregated in the lower levels of pay, power and prestige. Patriarchal sex-role stereotypes of women's nature and proper role which equate these with a domestic and service function continue to be seen as the underlying cause.

Gráinne O'Flynn and her classmates in a Dublin convent secondary school in the 1950s knew what was expected of them by parents, teachers and society. They were expected to find personal fulfilment and to make their contribution to society in the role of wife and mother. Marriage was a full-time career for women and all that was needed in addition was a nice job to fill the gap between schooldays and wedding day. This future domestic role was linked in their educators' mind with the idea of a limited range of human experience as suitable or necessary for girls. The managers of convent schools saw too great an interest in intellectual development or careers as a potential threat that might divert girls from their true vocation. In spite of this, female sexuality was not celebrated and fostered as the basis of this vocation. Instead it was presented in a strangely negative light. Girls were taught to see the female body primarily as an occasion of sin for males. Girls' responsibility to their sexuality was limited to playing it down in the interests of preserving their own and boys' purity. Prayer, modesty, low vocal tones and the avoidance of argument were recommended strategies. O'Flynn draws a vivid and entertaining picture of the contradictory messages she received about intellectual development when she recalls the conflict between her enthusiasm for Catholic apologetics and the stricture that to argue was unfeminine. She then examines the model of femininity 'presented to her' and her friends in the context of current feminist theology and finds the model to be fundamentally flawed.

Maria Slowey's study of women in adult education in 1977–8 looks at a group of women some of whom were probably contemporaries of O'Flynn's schoolgirls of the 1950s. She looked at the pattern of their choices from among the courses on offer within the formal adult educational system at a period just before the later development of women's self-directed learning projects. Most of the women chose courses which enhanced domestic skill or which had a cultural orientation. Very few opted for vocational courses. Slowey was particularly interested in the vocabulary used by the women to explain their choices. The words they used asserted their primary self-identification as women 'in the home'. This identification located 'the home' as apart from 'the world' into which other family members ventured each day and from which they returned to the home. The women saw their course as an 'outside interest', or a break or a change from home. Slowey sees this vocabulary as serving a purpose. She argues that it legitimates some level of dissatisfaction with full-time domesticity but at the same time allows the retention of a primary self-perception as a women permanently in the home. She sees it as providing a safety valve for frustration and as diffusing tensions which might otherwise lead to serious questioning of full-time, permanent domesticity.

Hannan and Breen's study of the next generation of school-girls finds the same paradigm at work. This is a study of sex-roles and education in a nationwide sample of second-level schools of all types in 1980. Its focus was on statistically significant differences in the proportions of girls and boys studying various subjects and on the causes underlying these differences. They found that the overall pattern of the girls' education was geared to preparation for an adult career as wife and mother in the home and to the needs of traditional areas of female employment. Expectations of different adult roles for boys and girls, within both marriage and employment, were shared by pupils, parents and teachers.

They also found another pattern of attitudes which was at least as powerful as conventional sex-role expectations in determining subject choices. Girls had significantly lower confidence in their own abilities, especially in science and mathematics, and were ambivalent as to the value of these and other 'difficult' subjects. Hannan and Breen concluded that changes in attitudes must come before there could be any real change in the pattern of subjects studied.

As well as directly demonstrating the strength and persistence of the patriarchal paradigm of male-female relationships these studies indirectly raise the further question: what kind of change does feminism want in education systems? It is clear that the differences between the educational experience of females and males is linked to the differences between the sexes in economic, social and political power and that this is not acceptable. After this things are not so clear. Ultimate objectives have to be established and strategies to achieve them devised. If the aim is an education that draws out the full human potential of both sexes it does not appear that there is so far any satisfactory blueprint. This in turn does not make the development of effective strategies any easier.

In the final chapter I take up some of these questions and suggest one approach from within the educational system. I question the effectiveness of concentrating feminist effort only on changing the hidden curriculum of attitudes and expectations of future adult roles unless this is supplemented by more attention to the overt content of the different subjects taught. Feminist scholarship has steadily established that much of the accumulated body of knowledge and theory passed on within the educational systems of western culture is knowledge and theory constructed within a patriarchal paradigm and permeated with sexist values which are the more powerful for being represented as value-free and 'human'. There is therefore a factual basis for the concept of 'boys' subjects' that relates to their actual content as well as to ideas of what it is appropriate for girls to study. This factual basis needs to be brought into the light and its identity declared and made known if girls and boys, and women and men, are to be in a position to recognise, and so to confront and challenge, one of the most powerful influences in their education.

It may be significant that it is in the personal recollections of O'Flynn and Cullen, rather than the organised surveys of Slowey and Hannan and Breen, that there is evidence of young girls' experiencing conflict between awareness of their potential and aspirations as individuals and awareness of social pressure to conform to a stereotype of feminity which rejects much of that potential and aspiration as unfeminine. This highlights the crucial importance of what is enquired about in social research and how closely it demands scrutiny.

Nuns in the Catholic Church in Ireland in the Nineteenth Century*

TONY FAHEY

The emergence and growth of female religious congregations was one of the strongest religious movements in nineteenth-century Catholic Europe. These congregations gave to
the church a new source of evangelising power and to women a
new form of involvement in life outside the home. In Ireland,
the number of nuns, most of them in newly founded congregations,[1] rose from 120 in 1800 to 1500 in 1851 and over 8000 in
1901 — a five-and-a-half fold increase in the second half of the
century alone.[2] In France there were about 12,000 nuns in
1808, 31,000 in 1831 and just short of 127,000 in 1878 — a four-
fold increase in the latter forty-seven years.[3] In Prussia between
1872 and 1906, the number of nuns increased more than three-
fold.[4] In the Netherlands, the number of convents rose from
seventy-two in 1850 to 423 in 1900 and the vocation rate more
than doubled in the same period.[5]

The nineteenth-century congregations, for the first time in
Christian history, made women more numerous than men in
full-time church service. From the early medieval era to the eve

1. Religious congregations are distinguished from religious orders mainly
   on the basis of the nature of their religious vows. Members of congregations take simple vows while members of orders take solemn vows
   (usually, in both cases, of poverty, chastity and obedience). The exact
   meaning of the distinction between solemn and simple vows has been
   disputed by theologians, but traditionally, the solemn vows of religious
   orders gave them a higher religious standing than was accorded to congregations. Strictly speaking, the term 'nun' refers to a member of a
   female religious order, the term 'sister' to a member of a congregation,
   through the distinction is not widely applied in everyday language.
2. Reports of a census of Catholic religious personnel in Ireland in 1800 are
   published in Charles Vane (ed), *Memoirs and Correspondence of Vis-
   count Castlereagh*, London: Henry Colborn, 1850, Vol. 4, pp 99–102,
   172. Data for 1851 and 1901 are from the Censuses of Population of Ireland in these years (Tables of Occupation).
3. Claude Langlois, 'Les effectives des congregations feminines au XIX
   siecle', *Revue d'Histoire de l'Eglise en France*, Vol. LX 1974, 56–7.
4. H. A. Krose, *Kirchliches Handbuch*, Freiburg: Herder, 1908, pp 183–4.
5. H. P. M. Goddijn, 'The sociology of religious orders and congregations', *Social Compass* 8, 5–6, 1960, pp 445–6.

of the French revolution, nuns typically numbered less than half the total of priests and monks.[6] In the course of the nineteenth century, the numbers of female religious rapidly overtook the numbers of priests and male religious. In Ireland in 1851, priests outnumbered nuns by 2500 to 1500. By 1901, the number of nuns, at over 8000, had jumped to more than double the number of priests (then at 3400) and almost seven times the number of men in religious brotherhoods (then at 1160).[7] Similarly in France: prior to the French revolution, nuns amounted to less than one-third of the total church establishment, but a century later their proportion had risen to 58 per cent.[8] In Prussia in 1906, nuns were 65 per cent of church personnel and in Bavaria, 63 per cent.[9] Throughout Europe generally, by the early twentieth century nuns had come to outnumber male religious and clergy of all kinds by something of the order of two to one.

These congregations which incorporated women into church service were a somewhat novel form of an ecclesiastical institution with a long and erratic history. Since the emergence of the earliest Christian communities, women had participated in the 'religious life', that is, in the pursuit of exceptional Christian virtue through systematic regimes of ascetic self-discipline. From the earliest days, the lives of 'consecrated virgins' were dominated by the imagery of divine bridehood. and as spouses of Christ they were directed to a more reclusive and devotional style of life than were male religious. In the middle ages, the nun's state, in principle at least, acquired an emphasis on the restrictive, non-utilitarian aspects of religious discipline — on the protection of physical and spiritual purity through a rigorous and often stifling regime of enclosure and on the denial to women of any ecclesiastical usefulness other than that afforded by prayer and divine adoration. Behind the theory, the reality of covent life up to the counter-reformation was one of occasional spiritual glories in the midst of an otherwise mixed record in which abuse and decay were as common

6. Christopher Brooke, *The Monastic World 1000–1300*, New York: Random House, 1974, pp 167–8.
7. *Censuses of Population*, Ireland, 1851 and 1901, Tables of Occupation.
8. Langlois, *op. cit.*, pp 62–3.
9. Krose, *op. cit.*, pp 175–6, 182–5.

as discipline, piety and respect, and righteous condemnation by reformers as common as public reverence.[10]

From the mid-seventeenth century, beginning with the setting up of Vincent de Paul's French Sisters of Charity, the movement to let female religious out of the cloister and into the world of practical pastoral service began to gain a hold in the church. Distinguished from the older female orders by their relative relaxation of cloister, their simple as opposed to solemn vows and their concern for public works of charity and evangelisation in place of a purely devotional life, the French Sisters of Charity represented a new type of female religious organisation. Over the seventeenth and eighteenth centuries, the church cautiously allowed a small number of new congregations of this type into existence. After 1800, however, the balance of favour between the traditional enclosed orders and the more open and active congregations switched rapidly in favour of the latter.[11] Although in theory the enclosed devotional life retained a higher spiritual value, in practice the church turned to the active religious and their services as useful sources of ecclesiastical vitality. By the end of the nineteenth century, the typical nun taught in public schools, visited the sick and the poor in their homes, worked in hospitals and provided other forms of welfare service, all in the cause of Catholic propagation. She was actively supported by the church and played an important role in its popular ministry. Although still oppressively secluded and restricted by present-day standards, the active sister of the nineteenth century was very transformed

10. Women in the religious life in the Middle Ages have attracted a good deal more scholarly attention from historians than have their counterparts of the nineteenth century. See, for example, Lina Eckenstein, *Women under Monasticism: Chapters on Saint-lore and Convent Life between A.D. 500 and A.D. 1500,* New York: Russell and Russell 1963 (first published 1896); Eileen Power, *Medieval English Nunneries c. 1275 to 1535,* New York: Biblio and Tanner 1960 (first published 1922); Ernest W. McDonnell, *The Beguines and the Beghards in Medieval Culture,* New York: Octagon Books 1969; Angela Lucas, *Women in the Middle Ages: Religion, Marriage and Letters,* Brighton: Harvester Press 1983.

11. For the institutional history of the female religious up to and during the nineteenth century see especially: Francis Callahan, *The Centralization of Government in Pontifical Institutes of Women,* Rome: Gregorian University 1948; M. Heimbucher, *Die Orden und Kongregationen der Katholischen Kirche,* Paderborn 1908; V. T. Schaaf, *The Cloister,* Cincinnati, Ohio: St Anthony Messenger 1921.

from the ideal of the enclosed devotional nun that prevailed in previous centuries.

Foundation of the Irish congregations

The pioneer of the new style of congregational life for women in Ireland was Honora ('Nano') Nagle, founder of the Presentation sisters in the 1770s. She was a lady of Catholic gentry stock from County Cork with a certain amount of independent wealth. A sojourn in Paris in her youth seems to have given her some experience of French experiments in the active female religious life, but she began her work on her own as a laywoman among the poor in the city of Cork in the 1750s. Over twenty years later, to give a broader range and continuity to her work, she gathered together a small group of women willing to take on the religious life, while at the same time working towards an all-purpose educational and social welfare service devoted entirely to the poor. It took a further twenty years for the group to obtain ecclesiastical approval and gain a secure footing in Cork. Lack of recruits, lack of money and a certain measure of public suspicion had hampered the new organisation in its earlier years and the great difficulties the group experienced in these areas indicate the novelty and pioneering character of their work. From the first decade of the nineteenth century, however, the Presentation order began to grow steadily and disseminate a new image of the female religious life to the popular Catholic imagination in Ireland.[12]

Following the success of the Presentation order after 1800, the rest of the major Irish foundations came quickly in the first half of the nineteenth century.[13] The Irish Sisters of Charity were founded in 1813 by Mary Aikenhead, the Loreto sisters in 1822 by Teresa Ball, and the Mercy sisters in 1831 by Catherine McAuley, all emerging in Dublin under the guidance of Archbishop Daniel Murray. The final important Irish foundation of the period was the Holy Faith sisters, founded in Dublin in

12. T. J. Walsh, *Nano Nagle and the Presentation Sisters* Dublin: M. H. Gill, 1959.
13. J. N. Murphy, *Terra Incognita, or the Convents of the United Kingdom,* London: Longmans 1876; A Member of the Congregation, *The Life and Work of Mary Aikenhead, Foundress of the Irish Sisters of Charity 1787–1858,* London: Longmans 1924; Sr Mary Bertrand Degnan, *Mercy Unto Thousands,* Dublin: Browne and Nolan, 1958; Roland Burke Savage, *Catherine McAuley, the First Sister of Mercy,* Dublin: Gill 1949.

1860 by Margaret Aylward. These foundations were complemented by Irish houses of congregations with continental
origins, as well as some adapted versions of female orders with
a more traditional heritage, to form the organisational base for
the rapid growth in overall numbers of female religious which
took place after 1850.

Following the European pattern, the Irish founders and
their early followers were typically devout laywomen from the
middle to upper layers of Catholic society, quite often with
independent wealth to devote to their religious efforts and
usually with sufficient social standing to gain them a hearing —
though often a reluctant one — from local clerical authorities.
Their spirituality was universally intense and usually involved
a strong impulse to traditional saintly asceticism. Any
tendencies towards reclusiveness and otherworldliness, however, were counterbalanced by a dedication to popular philanthropy. This philanthropy was very much marked by the
emerging bourgeois concern, in both Protestant and Catholic
circles, for the moral and spiritual degeneracy of the lower
orders, particularly in the growing commercial and industrial
towns and cities. The Catholic version, like the Protestant, was
strongly religious in substance, emphasising divine salvation as
the primary good for the deprived masses and religious instruction and strict moral training as the principal means to that
good. It had important mundane aspects as well, however,
since it regarded literacy, personal discipline and bourgeois
standards of respectability as the foundations of popular moral
and spiritual training. In disseminating their message, few of
the early religious founders started out with an interest in or
good opinion of the missionary usefulness of the female
religious life, since the versions of that life known at the time
were those of the closed devotional convent rather than the
missionary force. Rather, pious middle-class philanthropy
among Catholic women first expressed itself in a voluntary
secular form, but as it struggled with the discontinuity, lack of
support and lack of system inherent in that approach, those
women who were to emerge as the early religious founders
gradually and cautiously, and indeed sometimes reluctantly,
moved towards accommodation with the supporting framework provided by the newer forms of the female religious tradition.

Important as the personalities and motivations of the

11

founders of the congregations are, they do not explain the developments which flowed from their work. Why did the dramatic upsurge of the nineteenth-century congregations occur and what did it represent? One reason was the new openness in the church towards pastoral activity of a particular sort by female religious, an openness which developed in a piecemeal, *ad hoc* fashion, but which was nevertheless firmly established by the mid-nineteenth century. The new approach grew out of need, as part of the church's struggle to adapt to the pressures of the pluralist political and religious environment of the nineteenth century. As churchly allegiance among the mass of the population of Catholic Europe became a matter of choice rather than of compulsory fact, the church turned to the female congregations as a new missionary force. The task of the congregations, first worked out among the urban poor, was to encourage popular religious support through the display of a practical, caring face of Catholicism to a hitherto neglected and often abused mass audience. The special dedication of the female congregations to popular education and health care was in tune with the new importance of a practical commitment to welfare as a foundation for the popular acceptability of the church: only a truly 'mother' church could remain a widely popular church. As women, the nuns were suited to tasks in this area that male religious and clergy, given the role definitions of the time, were not. In dealing with children and the sick, and in taking (in theory at least) a nurturing, motherly approach to their problems, nuns added a new dimension to pastoral care. Consequently, in the urbanising, industrialising world of the nineteenth century, as the home, the family and the local community gained a new importance in church interest, nuns became new agents of church penetration into these areas and were increasingly in demand in the church to perform that task.

The relaxation of the traditionally very reclusive rules of cloister was the principal sign of the church's new attitude. This relaxation was not only a practical necessity required by the nature of active pastoral work. It also signalled the church's willingness to allow to women a capacity for moral self-control and spiritual growth through a limited contact with the world that traditional cloister regulations had implicitly long denied. The simpler cloister rules that were retained in the new congregations of the nineteenth century were not only less restrictive, they also reflected a different view of the meaning of convent life. The medieval view of the cloister as a prison for the passions, a means to control and subdue women's disorderly impulses, receded before the idea of the convent as a shelter, protective without being totally reclusive, more concerned with providing a supportive base for practical service than with keeping the lid on disruptive impulses. In spiritual life, the traditional ideal of the nun as spouse or spiritual lover gave ground to the more pragmatic notion of the nun as handmaid of the Lord, a servant to the pastoral work of the church. This shift no doubt lightened the spiritual atmosphere of the convent — the nineteenth-century congregations produced none of the strong manifestations of religious excitement that had been the stuff of the female religious life of earlier centuries. It also brought the life of the convent closer in tone to that of the outside world, particularly the world of the orderly middle-class women in her home. The concern with practical service in the nineteenth-century convent, especially as that concern was geared to the nurture of children, gave the convent a resonance with the lives of ordinary mothers that the enclosed, devotional havens of the traditional orders had avoided as a matter of spiritual principle.

In a number of ways, therefore, the nineteenth-century convent was structured to attract women and the flow of entrants throughout the Catholic church in that period is in part a measure of the success of the design. But the draw on its own does not explain why so many women were available and willing to respond to it. There is an additional question about the context which fostered the 'supply side' of congregational growth. In a general way, in Ireland at least, the growth of supply may well be accounted for in terms largely similar to those applied to the growth of the Catholic church as a whole. The material base for the church, including the congregations, was the Catholic farming and commercial middle class which generally prospered in the course of the nineteenth century in Ireland. The moral and devotional culture propagated by the church was linked in various ways to the interests and world views of that class, so that the growth of Catholicism was the cultural counterpart of the 'embourgeoisement' of the Irish class structure. Catholicism also provided a key element in emerging nationalist sentiment and mythology and so acquired a powerful leverage in the nationalist population.[14] The supply of women to the female congregations, therefore, can be seen as part of a more general social trend towards support of the church which emerged in the course of the nineteenth century.

But beyond these general explanations (which, of course, apply to Ireland and so may be of little help in explaining the parallel growth of congregations in the rest of Europe), we have little of the information necessary for a more detailed analysis of the growth of congregations. Although we have general statistics on the number and spread of nuns and some impressionistic information on their general social character, we know little of the family backgrounds, social class backgrounds, geographic origins or educational attainments of those who chose the religious life. A particular gap in our knowledge of the socio-economic character of the convent is the lack of information that has survived on lay sisters, that is, the lower ranking sisters, poorly educated and from poorer circumstances, who served as domestics and general servants in the convents. Lay sisters, as the menials of the convent, attracted even less attention than the average choir sister, herself rarely in the limelight, and so are even more shadowy figures in the history of the congregations. (Since the second Vatican council the distinction between lay sisters and choir sisters has been abolished, though the memory of the traditional exploitation and sometimes abuse of lay sisters in convents remains as a guilty memory among female congregations to the present.) Even in the case of the choir sister, there is much that it is very hard to discover, such as, for example, the nature and extent of the dowry system which was important for the social make-up as well as the economic viability of the convent. It is possible that an important factor in the popularity of the new congregations over the older female orders was that they had rather more modest pretensions to social status, and thus they expected less by way of dowries or status qualifications from incoming members. However, the extent of populism in recruitment to the new congregations is something that yet remains to be explored.

In looking for the attention of women in the growing

---

14. See, e.g. Emmet Larkin, 'Church, state and nation in modern Ireland', *American Historical Review* 80, 5, 1975; John A Murphy, 'The support of the Catholic clergy, 1750–1850,' *Historical Studies* 5, 1965; Eugene Hynes, 'The Great Hunger and Irish Catholicism', *Societas* 8, 1978.

Catholic middle classes in Ireland, the congregations experienced little competition from elsewhere. To be a nun was one of the few acceptable occupational outlets outside marriage and motherhood available to women of respectable background. In Ireland in the nineteenth century many women worked as domestic servants, dressmakers, milliners, spinners and weavers, as well as unpaid help in family farms or businesses. But if a woman aspired to something above menial service or semi-skilled labour, she had little choice but to become either a nun or a teacher, both then just emerging as female professional-level occupations. In 1861, the census of population in Ireland reported almost 8900 female teachers (Catholic and Protestant) as opposed to 2609 nuns. The only other sizeable female professional group was the 492 midwives.[15] By the end of the century, however, nuns had become, among Catholic women, the largest grouping in the census 'professional class'. In 1911, there were 8887 nuns, 8500 Catholic women teachers, 790 Catholic midwives, 621 certified Catholic nurses, as well as 2513 Catholic women in 'subordinate medical services', then included as a professional category. The only other Catholic female group of any size included in this category was the 1858 women employed as 'officers and clerks' in the civil service.[16] Thus the nuns were the biggest segment of the professional field for Catholic women, small as that field was.

The competition offered to the congregations by the life of wife and mother may not have been strong either. The requirements of chastity, childlessness and the disciplined life of the convent no doubt dimmed the attractions of the nun's life for many women, but for others these disadvantages may have seemed no more unappealing than the uncertain pleasures of marriage. It is possible to argue, of course, that the secular alternative that many nuns might have had to face was more likely to have been spinsterhood than marriage. In Ireland at least there was a rough correspondence between the rising vocation rate and the falling rate of marriage among women. However, it may be misleading to see cause and effect in this correspondence (if only because it did not hold in most other countries where the female vocation rate rose as fast as or faster than in Ireland). The religious vocation was a phenomenon of

15. *Census of Population 1861*, General Report, Appendix Table III.
16. *Census of Population 1911*, General Report, Table 20.

late adolescence rather than mature adulthood. Most nuns would have entered the religious life in their late teens and early twenties, too early to have lost hope of the chance of finding a husband, even if such a hope had ever been uppermost in their minds, by the time of entry. This means, for one thing, that the principal element in marriage patterns that would have been likely to affect vocations was not so much the rate of non-marriage (high only in exceptional cases like Ireland) as the preservation of even a slight delay of marriage beyond the teen-age years (common throughout the European middle classes). Such a delay would crucially extend the years of flux that occupied the gap between physical maturity and social matur-ity in the young person's life. Since the air around was strongly laced with the odours of sanctity, it was scarcely surprising that those years should so often end in the misty but emotionally enticing ground of the religious vocation.

There are other factors linked to the increase of female voca-tions which can only be briefly mentioned here. An obvious one is the spread of education among women, which made it possible to familiarise ever wider groups with the ideals and imagery of the religious life. As the convents themselves were major agents of educational growth, they thus provided a large part of their own machinery of expansion. Furthermore, the congregations were urban institutions, and in Ireland they grew where the towns grew (particularly the bigger towns and cities such as Dublin, Cork, Limerick, Galway and even Belfast, though gradually many smaller country towns also came to have convents). This is not to say that the majority of vocations came from towns, rather that, wherever they origin-ated (and that is uncertain), their work was tied to urban settings. The emphasis on community life meant that nuns never worked alone and rarely travelled far from their con-vents, so the sight of nuns in rural areas was a rarity. The association with towns was undoubtedly in part an association with commercial or industrial wealth — the survival of con-vents was always dependent on the availability of sufficient economic surplus for their support. The congregations grew fastest in those counties with an industrial or commercial economic base (such as Dublin, Cork and Louth) and were less prominent in even the more prosperous agricultural counties (such as Kildare and Meath). The regional unevenness in the growth of the congregations is suggested by the fact that, in the

1911 census, there were, relative to Catholic population, more than twice as many nuns recorded in Leinster as in Connaught — 38.3 nuns per 10,000 Catholics in Leinster as opposed to 17.8 nuns per 10,000 Catholics in Connaught.[17]

Nuns and education

Above all else, in Ireland as elsewhere, the new nuns of the nineteenth century were educators, and their most important social effects were achieved through the school system which they created. Outside of schooling, nuns were prominent in hospital development and nursing,[18] in the care of orphans and homeless girls, in the reform of 'fallen women', and in modest attempts to train and sometimes employ girls in occupations such as domestic service, weaving or clothes-making. But the bulk of their energies were devoted to schooling, and especially to popular elementary schooling for girls and infant boys.

The founders of the Irish congregations, especially Nano Nagle and Catherine McAuley, regarded the education of children as the central plank of their philanthropy and the church reinforced this commitment with the religious obligation to propagate the Catholic gospel in their work. However, the development of convent education was shaped not only by the nuns themselves and the church interests they represented, but also by the general nineteenth-century growth of mass elementary schooling. By participating in that growth, nuns strengthened the Catholic church's hand in education and so helped secure its position in nineteenth-century Ireland; they brought schooling to women and so affected the changing relationships of the sexes. More generally, however, they helped to develop and to extend to all the population the notion of long-term formal schooling as a necessity of childhood and a proper preparation for adult society. In this they linked themselves to the secular project of social organisation, integrating mass populations into orderly, well-disciplined societies and cohesive nation states. As champions of Catholicism, nuns entered into some conflict with anti-Catholic or simply non-Catholic

17. A. Fahey, *Female Asceticism in the Catholic Church: a case-study of nuns in Ireland in the nineteenth century.* Unpub. PhD thesis, University of Illinois, 1981, pp 66–76.

18. In Germany, nuns in health care outnumbered nuns in education (see H. A. Krose, *Kirchliches Handbuch* Freiburg: Herder 1908, pp 180ff). Elsewhere, as far as I know, the balance was the other way around.

social forces, but as disseminators of a particular form of social and personal discipline and manners, and as champions of a particular ideal of femininity and women's place in society, they were very much in tune with the trends of their times. The development of convent primary schooling in Ireland is in this sense a good illustration of the peculiar mix of churchly idealism and mundane realism which characterised the success of the female congregations in the nineteenth century.

In Ireland, nuns had little impact on public education in the first quarter of the nineteenth century and not much more in the second. They had begun to enter elementary education since the earliest part of the century, but in spite of Catholic–Protestant tensions in this area and in spite of the state's concern with education, and particularly with the issue of sectarianism in elementary schools, little attention was paid to the nuns' work before 1850. In the 1830s, convent schools began to apply for admission into the newly established National Education system. The National Education Commissioners readily accepted them and no Protestant watchdog bodies cried alarm at their decision.[19]

The relaxed reaction to convent schools in the 1820s, 1830s and 1840s among groups normally anxious about Catholic educational expansion reflected the smallness of convent numbers and the scarcity of their schools. In 1824–5, there were a mere forty-six convent elementary schools, as opposed to 919 Kildare Place schools, over 1000 schools run by Protestant bodies, as well as myriad hedgeschools, so that the congregations were still relatively unknown as Catholic educational forces.[20] Furthermore, dominant opinion in the early nineteenth century still held that teaching was properly a male domain: the rural hedgeschools were almost universally run by male teachers and the early National Education Commissioners, keeping up this tradition, declared their intention of using female teachers only for 'sewing, or knitting, or platting straw, or other female work'.[21]

19. *Report of the Select Committee appointed to inquire into the progress and operation of the plan of education in Ireland,* H.C. 1837 [485] IX, pp 50–51.
20. *Second Report of the Commissioners of Enquiry on Irish Education,* H.C. 1826–27 (2) XII, pp 46–7.
21. *Report of the Royal Commission of Enquiry into Primary Education in Ireland* (Powis Commission) H.C. 1870 XXVIII, pt 1, p. 45.

However, from the 1820s, the number of convent national schools and pupils grew steadily. By 1853 there were 104 convent schools in the National Education system and by 1910 there were 345. These schools represented a relatively small proportion of all national schools (2.2 per cent in 1853, 4.1 per cent in 1910) but they incorporated a substantially larger proportion of the school population (11 per cent of average daily attendance in 1853, 17 per cent in 1910).[22] These figures mean that by the end of the nineteenth century something less than one in three of Catholic girls and about one in ten of Catholic boys who attended national schools were in convent schools.[23] By that time also, however, the convent schools had acquired an importance in this field of education greater even than their weight in schools and pupils would suggest. From about the middle of the century, in both Protestant and Catholic circles and from a secular as well as religious viewpoint, convent schools had begun to win an image of themselves as cornerstones of popular education in Ireland, and so acquired a symbolic as well as a practical prominence in the educational field.

An important basis for the convent schools' image was the material one: in a national education system given very meagre support from state funds, convents were able to attract the financial support from the Catholic faithful to provide the model schools of the system. One estimate calculated that between 1800 and 1868, in twenty-six of Ireland's twenty-eight dioceses, 217 convents had been built at a cost of over one million pounds, which represented an expenditure per convent that was almost three times what was then spent on building the average Catholic church.[24] The elementary schools attached to these convents included some of the biggest and best equipped in the system and the general run of convent schools was far superior in basic architectural terms to the

22. 1853 was the first year in which the annual report of the Commissioners of National Education gave statistical information on convent schools as distinct class in the National system. The practice was continued through to the final report in 1919.
23. In 1901, about one-fifth of convent school pupils at the primary level were boys — infant boys mainly (see *Census of Population 1901*, General Report, Tables of Educational Establishments, pp 164–5).
24. E. Larkin, 'Economic growth, capital investment and the Roman Catholic church in nineteenth-century Ireland', *American Historical Review* 72, 3 (April 1967), p. 874.

miserly two- and three-room schools that served as the standard for ordinary pupils.[25] As with capital costs, the convent schools were largely self-supporting or effective at gathering voluntary aid for their day-to-day running costs. Although in principle entitled to the same level of state building grants and teachers' salaries as all other national schools, convents balanced independence against the available state largesse and so ended up rejecting much of the state aid. In particular, nuns refused to take the state examinations required for classification as salaried teachers and were paid instead on a capitation basis per pupil rather than by means of a straight salary. As a result, by the 1870s cost to the state per nun teaching in convent schools attached to the national system was on average about one-third that of lay teachers in ordinary schools (in 1874, the average salary paid by the National Board to lay teachers was less than £37, compared to £13 for the average nun).[26] Consequently, the large teaching corps provided by the congregations possessed the great virtue in nineteenth-century social service in Ireland of costing very little to the central administration.

The financial vitality of the convent system was matched by the social and cultural solidity of the nuns and their educational style. Primarily, the teaching congregations viewed their teaching duties in religious terms. Thus, for example, the Presentation constitution defined the special goal of that order as 'the instruction of poor female children in the principles of Religion and Christian piety'.[27] But the public perception of the sisters went far beyond an appreciation of their piety. They were also seen as paragons of educated bourgeois femininity, a view which has come down to us especially through the reports of the national school inspectorate. One inspector, writing in 1864 of a convent of Mercy school in Athy, reported that 'most of the nuns get a liberal education of a high order and are highly accomplished; some draw and paint admirably, and

25. *Special report made to the Commissioners of National Education on convent schools in connection with the Board,* H.C. 1864 (405) XLVI, pp 51, 64, 73; *Thirty-first report of the Commissioners of National Education,* H.C. 1865 [3496] XIX, Appendix A, p 8.
26. *Return of grants made by the Irish National Education Board to convent and monastic schools for 1863, 1864, and 1874...,* H.C. 1875 (451) LIX, p 341.
27. *Rules and Constitutions of the Religious Sisterhood of the Presentation of the Ever Blessed Virgin Mary.* Cork: Frances Guy 1859.

know music and French; others know music and French [sic], having been educated in France'.[28] Other inspectors' comments from the same period are similar. In a Mercy convent in Armagh, all the nuns 'have received the education of ladies'; in the Mercy convent in Ennis 'the acquirements of the nuns, so far as a lady's education is concerned, are very high'; of the Poor Clares in Belfast, 'their acquirements are ladylike and such as would be expected of persons in their position'; in the Stradbally Presentation convent in Offaly '[the nuns] received a liberal education, being members of responsible and some of them very high families; this would be seen at once from their manner and address'.[29]

Giving a practical impetus to the sisters' ladylike manners was their energy in bringing their educational message to their schoolchildren, and particularly to the children of the lower orders who proved so resistant to every other avenue of middle-class influence. Nineteenth-century society was impressed and grateful at the sight of nuns taking on with determination and energy the odious task of gentling and training the unwashed throng.

> The social position of the ladies of the convent, their acknowledged capabilities as teachers, the disinterestedness and their high religious character, added to their constant and regular visitation of parents and pupils have such an attractive influence on the Roman Catholic poor, that numbers are brought under their instruction who otherwise would be brought up in ignorance and vice. The good effected in this way, as compared to ordinary schools, cannot be overestimated.[30]

The school inspectorate readily gave credit to the teaching nuns for their role in the expansion of mass literacy which was the most evident achievement of the national school system. It is doubtful whether the educational parity between girls and boys at the primary level (and the higher standard frequent among girls) which was maintained throughout the nineteenth century in Ireland could have been managed without the

28. *Special report made to the Commissioners of National Education on convent schools in connection with the Board,* H.C. 1864 (405) XLVI, p. 124.
29. *Ibid.,* pp 7, 14, 23, 59, 187.
30. *Ibid.,* p. 8.

efforts of the convent schools. But educational officialdom was equally impressed by the nuns' success in their more general civilising mission, especially in the 'moral instruction' of the poor and unruly. One inspector reported on a recently opened convent school:

> When I visited the (convent) school shortly after its opening, the girls were in the rudest possible state, boisterous, disobedient, and impudent, the greater part of whose time had been spent running almost wild in the streets. I now find these girls quite amenable to discipline and order, somewhat attentive to neatness and propriety, and generally improved in moral training.[31]

The message of this and numerous similar assessments was not lost on the educational authorities when the growth and success of convent education began to arouse some opposition from Protestant critics in the 1850s and 1860s, leading to sporadic Protestant campaigns to have the National Board disavow its association with convent schools. Seeking an explanation for the success of these schools, groups of Protestants, particularly in the Presbyterian strongholds of Ulster, looked not to the internal strengths of the teaching congregations but to the harassment and dictation of the Catholic clergy and behind that even to the conniving sympathies of the Dublin administration. Whatever about their views on the conspiratorial nature of the Catholic church, Protestant critics were not far wrong in their views of the sympathies of the Dublin administration.[32] In 1854, Maurice Cross, secretary to the National Education Commissioners (and an Anglican), had stated in defence of convent schools to a lords' enquiry that such schools 'present generally the best specimens of education that Ireland can produce'.[33] Ten years later, in response to a further wave of Protestant attack, the national school inspectorate produced a highly favourable survey and analysis of the convent schools in the national system, and the National

31. *Ibid.,* p. 218.
32. Extensive documentation arising from a controversy over convent schools in the National system is collected in H.C. 1864 XLVI (this volume of the Parliamentary Papers forms the most comprehensive source on convent elementary schools in the 1850s and early 1860s).
33. *Report of the Lords' committee on the practical working of the system of National Education in Ireland* H.C. 1854 XV, p. 107.

Education Commissioners, in an indirect but nonetheless remarkable admission of the weakness of their own system declared that, for the diffusion of education, the national system needed convent schools more the the convent schools needed the national system.[34]

By the time of the Powis Commission investigations into education in 1868–70, the strengthening image of the teaching congregations among educational officialdom had become clearcut, amounting almost to an implicit official credo in the educational superiority of convent schools. By then, in contrast to the position of fifty years previously, the congregations were viewed, not as peculiar hangovers from the medieval Catholic church, nor even as partisan defenders of Catholic church interests (though undoubtedly they were that), but as exemplars of the new secular practice of mass popular schooling.[35] Their labour came cheap, which the National Education Commissioners were quite ready to acknowledge as a virtue, all the more so because of the high social standing of the nuns. The quiet satisfaction of the state educational authorities with the performance of convent schools also suggested that the nuns' work was channelled in the right direction as far as the authorities were concerned. While the nuns' educational message was not overtly political, its emphasis on 'moral instruction' taught a respect for civilised convention and through that a respect for established authority, both civil and religious. Unlike the overtly nationalist Christian Brothers, the nuns did not figure as opponents in the educational field of the Anglocentric tendencies of the national school curricula. Their concern for the Gaelic past or the Irish language was slow to develop and their cultural leanings, where they had any distinctiveness, tended more towards a provincial fondness for French literary polish. Otherwise, to judge by reports of the school inspectorate, they pursued the embourgeoisement of Irish culture with missionary conviction, struggling to raise the tone of Irish life to the civilised standards of metropolitan culture. Consequently, although occasionally bemused by the archaic accoutrements

34. *Revised rules recently sanctioned by the Commissioners of National Education – Dissents from, or Protests against the adoption of any of the above rules...*, H.C. 1864 (157) XLVI p. 39.
35. See, e.g. *Report of the Royal Commission of Enquiry into Primary Education in Ireland* (Powis Commission) H.C. 1870 XXVIII, pt 3, pp 67–68, 163–4, 188, 248–9, 707.

of ritual and habit that surrounded the nuns' lives, non-Catholic liberal opinion of this period readily looked on the Catholic nun as the ideal teacher for the popular elementary school.

A major prize won by the nuns in the nineteenth-century educational war, and one that testified more than any other to their prominence in elementary education, was the control ceded to them by the state authorities over teacher training for Catholic women. From the 1830s, the National Board had struggled somewhat more consistently to retain a direct control in this field than it had in many others. Through its own non-denominational teacher training colleges it had attempted to counteract some of the spirit of denominational separatism which had permeated the national schools. The effort gradually crumbled as Catholic school managers (nearly always local clergy or religious) refused to engage the products of the 'godless' state training colleges. For Catholic girls' schools, the convents competed with the Board's colleges as a source of supply for teachers: by the 1870s, over three-quarters of Catholic female lay teachers were officially untrained, which in fact meant that a large proportion of them had received an unofficial and largely informal training as monitors in convent schools.[36] The National Board had not helped its own cause by subventing the monitorial system with (albeit small) annual grants for the payment of monitors, a subvention which benefited convent schools and their monitorial training disproportionately.[37] In the 1880s the National Board gave up the struggle: it established a new system of wholly denominational teacher training institutes, with the Mercy convent in Baggot Street (later moved to Carysfort) as the main institute for Catholic women. Thus the Mercy sisters were given control over the main avenue of access to the teaching profession at primary level for Catholic women.

36. *Letter from the Chief Secretary to the National Education Commissioners,* H.C. 1875 (70) LIX, p. 11.
37. *Return of grants made by the Irish National Education Board to convent and monastic schools for 1863, 1864, and 1874 ...,* H.C. 1785 (451) LIX, pp 1–3, 340–41; cf also, for inspectors' comments on the role of the monitorial system as an unofficial teacher training system, *Special report made to the Commissioners of National Education on convent schools in connection with the Board,* H.C. 1864 (405) XLVI, pp 16–17, 32, 34, 41, 45–7, 74, 101, 136.

The setting up of the teacher training institute at Baggot Street was part of the gradual feminisation of the teaching profession in the nineteenth century (by 1890 over half of the national school teachers were women, compared to 28 per cent in 1835).[38] Convent schools no doubt contributed to this process, though perhaps no more than did the low rate of pay which reduced the attraction of the profession for men. However, the prominence won by convents in teacher training had its limits, reflecting some of the more general limits imposed on the congregations' impact on the world by a decidedly non-intellectual, if not anti-intellectual, orientation to their roles. In general, nineteenth-century female congregations showed little interest in developing an academic or technical dimension to their work. National school inspectors repeatedly faulted nuns for failing to undertake formal training. The paradox by which nuns were nevertheless regarded as the best teachers and eventually became important trainers of teachers themselves reflected the technical underdevelopment of the teaching profession rather than the highly professional approach of nuns. Despite their importance in education, nuns made no contribution to the science of pedagogy. Outside of catechetics, they presented no independent viewpoint on the underlying principles or philosophy of the curricula they taught and so, despite their practical experience, made little contribution to formal educational thought. To my knowledge, they wrote no school textbooks. In the teacher training institute in Baggot Street the technical subjects such as science and mathematics were taught by lay males, while the nuns confined themselves to the accomplishment subjects like singing, music and foreign languages. Among the teaching posts listed for the institute in the 1890s, pedagogy had no place.[39]

Nuns in this period clearly believed that excellence in teaching was a product of devotion, care and good basic education rather than of technical training. (A similar non-technical approach seems to have been very strong in their work in health care where, especially in nursing and hospital management, nuns introduced progress through diligence, care and

38. *Fifty-seventh annual report of the Commissioners of National Education for the year 1890,* H.C. 1891 XXI, pp 45–6.
39. *Returns relating to National Education in Ireland...,* H.C. 1892 (335) LXI, pp 237–40.

order in daily routines rather than through the development and acquisition of formal professional skills.)[40] They were enthusiastic and effective practitioners of such occupational skills as were readily available in their fields in the nineteenth century, and the capable labour which their members supplied enhanced their impact in those fields, but in their anti-technical attitudes they were more like keen amateurs than professionals in the strict sense of the term.

Nuns and the position of women

The work of nuns in the nineteenth century was work geared primarily to the world of women and provided a mirror to the limitations and strengths of that world. (Even in hospitals where nuns worked with male doctors and male as well as female patients, their principal public function was to perform the feminine role of nursing and human support in the technical and impersonal world of professionalised medicine.) The position of nuns in the church echoed the position of women in the home — essential but subordinate. Congregations founded in the nineteenth century ranked low on the ecclesiastical pyramid: they were denied not only the dignity of holy orders but even the triple solemn vows of the nuns of earlier centuries. Their tasks remained within the traditional women's sphere of caring and nurturing — tending to the sick, teaching simple religious truths to the poor and to children, training older girls in modesty and industry. These activities complemented the pastoral work of the clergy but they stayed far removed from university training and scholarly work, from the higher reaches of church administration and from the larger issues of theology, politics and overall development which occupied the church as a whole. Consequently, while the role for women in the church established by these sisters was new and in missionary terms important, and while it offered a widely followed occupational outlet for women, it was far from shattering the limitations imposed on women in the Catholic tradition.

However, while it is obvious that nuns were not overt champions of women's rights in the modern sense, it is less obvious what their long-term impact on the social position of

40. *Report of the committee of inquiry into the management and working of the hospitals of the City of Dublin,* H.C. 1887 [c.5042] XXXV, pp xxxi–xxxv.

women was. The church's increasing utilisation of the pastoral labours of the female congregations could be viewed as the tip of a much broader transformation of the position of women in the church's lay support. As the world of men — the world of politics, economic life, intellectual life — became increasingly secularised, the world of women — the home and domestic life — attracted a new sacralisation. The prayerful family, led by the mother, became the bastion of the faith while the world outside wandered from the true path. The new role accorded nuns, then, could be seen as a parallel to a new position allowed to women generally. Medieval thinking on women, especially in clerical circles, had been preoccupied with the image of Eve, the scheming seductive temptress. The medieval church's struggle to extend a monkish respect for chastity and celibacy outside of the monastery to all the clergy had extended with it a tortured misogyny, born of endless sexual temptation, that had ravaged the male monastic tradition. By the nineteenth century, however, the Christian churches had developed a less overtly hostile and dismissive attitude towards the female sex. The Victorian ideology of women's 'passionlessness' presented women as creatures without sexual desire, in strong contrast to the often lurid medieval imagery of female lust and animality.[41] The Victorian idealisation of the pure and sexless woman, in its Catholic as well as its Protestant manifestations, transformed women from creatures of carnal evil to repositories of moral good and in the process, among its many other ramifications, brought the woman's sphere closer to the centre of religious attention.

We have had little detailed analysis of how the position of women in Ireland was affected by religious culture, much less how that position was affected by the mediation of nuns. Historians such as Nancy Cott and Ann Douglas have argued that in nineteenth-century America, the elevation of women's position in the lay support of the Protestant churches contributed to the nineteenth-century cult of domesticity and indirectly formed a source of strength for women, despite its

41. Nancy Cott, 'Passionlessness: an interpretation of Victorian sexual ideology, 1790–1850' *Signs* 4, 2 (Winter) 1978.

limitations.[42] We could speculate that something broadly similar occurred as part of the role played by women in Irish Catholicism. One could suggest that it was primarily as wife and mother that the Irish Catholic church drew on and utilised the support of the laywoman, and that the church in return propped up and glorified those roles. The common image that we have of the Catholic mother is one of a devout woman, temperate and restrained, thoroughly loyal to her faith and her church, and quite often self-consciously more pious than the typical male. Within the home, however, she also appears as a moralising woman, going beyond passive acceptance of priestly direction to an active and highly effective reproduction of Catholic religious culture in her children, often in the face of her husband's indifference or remoteness. It was in her role as moral and spiritual guide to her children, and to a lesser extent as moral influence on her husband, that she was the counterpart in the Catholic laity of the nineteenth-century nun. Indeed, to pursue the parallels with Protestantism, one could usefully compare and contrast the role in women's religious culture of the Catholic nun and the Protestant clergyman's wife (though the missionary scope of the celibate nun was vastly the greater of the two). One would wonder also by how much the sanctified chastity of the nun differed in symbolic impact from the wifely purity of the Protestant ideal for women. For Catholic women, whether nun or lay, the confessional provided perhaps the major religious lifeline but its role in women's lives remains a private and hidden realm of history. (It is intriguing to remember, though, that the access to women's inner lives provided to priests in the confessional was an important cause of male anti-clericalism in some Catholic countries, and was a source of horrified fascination to nineteenth-century Protestantism.)[43]

Given the many areas that remain obscure in the nexus of women and religion in Catholicism, we are thrown back to speculation to try to summarise the impact of nuns on the

42. Nancy Cott, *The Bonds of Womanhood. 'Women's Sphere' in New England, 1780–1835,* New Haven: Yale University Press 1977; Ann Douglas, *The Feminization of American Culture* New York: Avon Books 1978.
43. J. Michael Phayer, *Sexual Liberation and Religion in Nineteenth-Century Europe* Totowa, New Jersey: Rowman and Littlefield 1977, Chap. 6. Jules Michelet, in his *Priests, Women and Families* (London 1845), presents an anti-clerical tract on this theme.

development of women's social status. One argument is that female piety was a tool of repression directed at women themselves by a male dominated religious tradition, and that this tool was rendered all the more effective by becoming more subtle and pervasive in the nineteenth century (as it did through nuns). A parallel argument is that the idealised domestic realm which grew up in conjunction with this peity and which seemed to honour women was in reality a cage gilded with the frills and flowery language of the cult of wifely and motherly honour.[44] An alternative view is that, however empty much of the rhetoric in praise of female honour and piety might be and however much it served the interests of male comfort and dominance, it gave real help to women to improve their education, strengthen their influence and develop a world of satisfactions of their own. A stronger version of this argument is that there was much in the ideology of women's sphere that came from women's own motives: that it provided a 'basis for a subculture among women that formed a source of strength and identity and afforded supportive sisterly relations' and that, in this sense, far from being a male-devised block to women's progress, it formed the early foundations of modern feminism.[45]

The conflicting realities reflected in these arguments were fully represented in the lives of nineteenth-century nuns and the lay women who looked to them as guides. On the one hand, the determined lowliness with which nuns viewed their lives in the church and their firm subordination to male ecclesiastics paralleled the subordination of women in general and marked it with the stamp of sacred approval. On the other hand, nuns enhanced the lives of women with education and practical social service and provided basic assistance and moral support to mothers in their struggles through childrearing and family life. In this role nuns were hailed and welcomed in their own day, by women at least as much as men, and in Ireland their schools and hospitals were looked to as havens of order and succour in a demoralised world. The life of the nun in itself offered an outlet for women and was taken to with energy by

44. J. Lee applies a variation on this approach to Ireland in his 'Women and the Church since the Famine' in M. MacCurtain and Donncha O'Corrain, (eds) *Women in Irish Society: the Historical Dimension,* Dublin: Arlen House 1978.
45. Nancy Cott, *Bonds of Womanhood,* p. 197.

thousands of dedicated women. In the end, simple judgements on the good or bad effected by nuns are impossible to make and are quite likely to be offered on too limited grounds where they are attempted. All we can say at present is that, where women and religion are concerned, they were central figures and deserve a closer attention from historians than they have received so far.

This paper is based on Ph.D research completed in 1981.

The Revolution in Girls' Secondary Education in Ireland 1860–1910

ANNE V. O'CONNOR

It is often assumed that the education of girls in Ireland was until recently totally inadequate, or at best a reinforcement of our stereotyped roles as wives and mothers. Yet the historical evidence suggests that by the beginning of the twentieth century *the* fundamental revolution had already taken place in the education of girls in Ireland. This was the provision of a system of education which gradually enabled girls to compete with boys in the public examination system and to obtain similar though less well paid employment.

New values and educational reform

This development could not have taken place without the profound social and economic changes which occurred in Irish society during the nineteenth century. The most important of these was the emergence of an Irish Catholic middle class, eager to gain its share of economic and political power. It was the growing strength and identity of this class that created, during the period 1880–1910, the beginnings of a new order, based on the values of an industrialised society.

These new values came from England, where the industrial revolution had ushered in an era of great social reform. The Reform Bill of 1832 had begun the process of enfranchising the middle class. Although women did not get the vote until the first decades of the twentieth century, the first petition for women's suffrage was presented to parliament in 1866, and the National Society for Women's Suffrage was founded in 1867.[1] Women also benefited from the fact that so many groups and classes were being freed from the restrictions of the past. The growing preoccupation with emancipation can be seen in the political writings of John Stuart Mill: he wrote *Liberty* in 1859 and *The Subjection of Women* in 1869.[2] Even though Mill's ideas on votes for women proved to be in advance of their time, yet the passing of the first Married Women's Property Act in

---

1. *The Englishwoman's Review,* n.s. XXXIX, 15 April 1908,p. 73.
2. John Stuart Mill, *Autobiography* (London 1873) pp 251, 265.

1870 was a clear indication that women's position in the family was changing dramatically.[3]

Educational reform in England in the mid-nineteenth century was part of a wider movement for economic and political freedom for women, and women's education came to be seen as a necessary prerequisite for jobs, rather than as a preparation for marriage.

By the 1860s this English view had reached Ireland, where it was at first confined to a small number of Protestant girls' schools in Dublin, Belfast, Cork and Mountmellick, which prepared girls to be governesses and teachers. The three names particularly associated with this reform movement were Margaret Byers, who founded the Ladies' Collegiate School (later Victoria College), Belfast, in 1859, Anne Jellicoe, whose major achievements were the establishment of the Queen's Institute (1861), Alexandra College (1866) and School (1873), Dublin, and Isabella Tod, who founded the Ladies' Institute, Belfast, in 1867, and who was the main influence behind the Ulster Head Schoolmistresses' Association, founded in 1880. This association worked closely with the Central Association of Irish Schoolmistresses and other Ladies interested in Irish Education, founded in 1882. Between them they represented approximately seventy Protestant girls' schools in Ireland, and exerted a great deal of influence in the 1880s at a crucial stage in the development of girls' secondary education when nuns could not join any association.

Both Byers and Jellicoe were primarily educationalists, interested in downgrading the accomplishments and raising the academic standard of girls' secondary and higher education. Anne Jellicoe does not fit into the mainstream of educational reformers of this period in the sense that she did not profess an interest in the wider questions of feminism and women's rights. The only women's right for which she contended was, to quote her own words, 'their right to be educated'.[4] Yet, through her involvement in bettering the condition of women in society, she was to play an important role in their emancipation.

She started by founding a lace embroidery school in Clara,

3. J. Lawson and H. Silver, *A Social History of Education* (London 1973) p. 341.
4. *The Englishwomen's Review,* n.x. XI, 15 Nov. 1880, pp 518–9.

Co. Offaly, in 1853 which lasted until 1856; helped to run a school for poor children in the Liberties area of Dublin between 1858 and 1861; visited the women prisoners in Mountjoy jail to report on conditions there; made a detailed study of the conditions under which young girls worked in Dublin factories in 1861; helped to found the Queen's Institute, Dublin, for the technical instruction of women in 1861, Alexandra College, Dublin, in 1866, the Governess Association of Ireland in 1869, and finally Alexandra School in 1873.[5] Her schemes were to contribute not only to the development of secondary education for girls, but also to the opening of the universities and professions for women. By the time she died in 1880 girls were allowed to enter for the Intermediate (second-level) examinations (started in 1879) and the first university clases were being started at Alexandra College for the degrees of the Royal University of Ireland.

Anne Jellicoe's major educational venture, Alexandra College, was modelled directly on Queen's College, Harley Street, London, the first college for the higher education of women in England, founded in 1848.[6] She had spent the years 1862–4 trying to persuade the citizens of Dublin of the need for a training college for governesses, but had met with no success until the arrival of Dr Chenevix-Trench as Church of Ireland Archbishop of Dublin in 1864. He had been personally involved in the running of Queen's College, London, for ten years, and suggested that she broaden the base of her new college by making it an institution for the higher education of girls, aged 15 years and over, based on the liberal principles of a University as at Queens College, London. His intervention was crucial as it ensured that the emphasis would be on a university-type education from the outset. With this in mind Alexandra employed professors from Trinity College, Dublin, to lecture the students (aged fifteen years and over) in a wide range of subjects, including theology, history, English, French, German or Italian, Latin, geography, arithmetic, algebra and geometry, natural science, philosophy, music, drawing and drill.[7]

5. Material obtained from Friends' Historical Library, 6 Eustace Street, Dublin.
6. Elaine Kaye, *A History of Queen's College, London,* 1848–1972 (London 1972), p. 88.
7. Printed Prospectus of Alexandra College, October 1867 (Archives, Alexandra College).

Some idea of the disapproval then current about Alexandra College can be gathered from the remarks of the Rev Pakenham Walsh about the college at the time of its foundation: 'In that College they would have professors to teach young ladies to cook a meal.'[8] In fact, by educating the future teachers at university level, especially in subjects such as Latin and mathematics, Alexandra College began the movement to reform girls' secondary education in Dublin. The inclusion of such subjects marked the real revolution in girls' secondary education in Ireland, for until women teachers were themselves educated to university level in academic subjects, there was no possibility of change in the curricula of girls' secondary schools. Advertisements for the period 1840–80 show that the majority of girls' schools included English, French, history, geography, use of the globes, writing, arithmetic, drawing, music and needlework in their school programme.

Margaret Byers was another pioneer working to reform girls' secondary education in Ireland. From a Presbyterian background, she was born in Rathfriland, Co. Down, in 1832 and educated in England.[9] Her marriage to the Rev John Byers brought her briefly to Princeton, New Jersey, USA, where she was deeply impressed by certain aspects of the American High School system of education, notably the idea that the education of boys and girls should be similar. She left for China with her missionary husband in 1852, but his death within a year left her a widow with an infant son. She returned to Ireland and became headmistress of a ladies' school in Cookstown, Co. Tyrone. She remained there for five years before setting up her own school in Belfast in 1859, under the name of the Ladies' Collegiate School (later Victoria College). Margaret Byers was highly critical of the girls' schools in Belfast during the twenty-year period prior to the introduction of the Intermediate Act of 1878, which established examinations for secondary pupils, including girls for the first time. Her main grounds of complaint centred around the following points: the time spent at even the best schools was so short that any intellectual development was difficult to achieve; the school curriculum was almost invariably limited to subjects which could be displayed in the

8. *Saunders Newletter and Daily Advertiser,* 28 March 1866.
9. Manuscript on the life of Mrs Margaret Byers, LL.D (1832–1912) by her son, Sir John Byers (Archives, Victoria College, Belfast).

drawing room; arithmetic and English grammar were usually given little attention in girls' schools; masters were usually employed for two or three hours a week to teach such subjects as arithmetic and English, thus admitting 'the inability of women to undertake these themselves'; resident English governesses were advertised in order to recommend schools to parents, although owing to the state of girls' education in England they were no better than the home-grown variety, except as regards accent.[10]

In her efforts to improve standards in her school Margaret Byers found it necessary at first to employ masters, many of whom were graduates of the Queen's University or the Presbyterian Assembly's College, and under their guidance examinations were introduced, some of them being set by professors of Queen's College, Belfast.[11] Students received certificates if they achieved a certain standard of answering (between 50 per cent and 75 per cent) in their examinations, while those above 75 per cent obtained prizes.[12] As a result the school was ideally placed to take advantage of the special examinations for women started by Queen's University in 1870, and Byers immediately sent in students from the two senior classes.[13] The effect of these university examinations on the work of the secondary school was already apparent by 1879, when Byers could state that every teacher on her staff (sixteen ladies and seven masters) many of whom were ex-students, possessed university certificates.[14]

In 1782 Margaret Byers helped to organise the first of many public meetings on girls' secondary and higher education in Belfast in conjunction with Mrs William Grey, the founder of the high school movement in England (1870).[15] The main features common to this new approach to girls' secondary education were great stress on public examinations as a means of raising standards, the inclusion of mathematics and Latin in the curriculum, a close liason between secondary schools and university, and the belief that the education of boys and girls should, as far as possible, be the same.

10. Minutes of evidence, Mrs M. Byers, before the Intermediate Education (Ireland) Commission. H.C. 1899/c.9512/XIII, p. 295.
11. *The Englishwomen's Review,* n.s. XI, 15 Nov. 1880, p. 312.
12. *The Northern Whig,* Belfast, 24 June 1875.
13. *Ibid.,* 29 June 1877.
14. *Ibid.,* 13 Oct. 1879.
15. *Ibid.,* 16 Jan. 1872.

The Catholic tradition of girls' education
The concepts involved in the high school movement clashed sharply with the views that had prevailed on girls' education in many Irish convent schools, which were influenced by the long-standing French religious tradition of girls' education. This tradition was based on a hierarchic view of society, which held to the view that girls' secondary education should diverge from that of boys, as their future lay in different directions. A girls' future role was seen within the family context, as wife and mother, with a corresponding emphasis on the accomplishments and social graces.

Dr Paul Cullen, the Roman Catholic archbishop of Dublin who exercised a powerful influence on the development of convent education in Ireland during the period 1852–78, put forward views in the early 1870s, which showed that he continued to adhere to these traditional ideas. When asked to support the high school movement in England, just then starting, his reply showed that he held the view that a woman's role in society still lay within the family structure, and that the whole emphasis should, therefore, be on the religious and domestic aspects of her education, rather than on the secular and public. This was in direct contrast to the high school movement, which urged that girls' education should be very similar to that of boys. In support of his views, Cullen quoted St Paul: 'Teach the young women to be wise, to love their husbands, to love their children; to be discreet, chaste, sober, having a care of the house, gentle, obedient to their husbands, that the word of God be not blasphemed.'[16]

Margaret Ann Cusack (the famous 'nun of Kenmare'), in an article called 'Woman's Place in the Economy of Creation' written in 1874, fully supported this view. She urged that women should be educated 'carefully, steadily and thoughtfully' with a grave sense of their future roles as wives and mothers. Their mission was a noble one and was not to attempt to rival men in professions unsuited to their sex nor to make a parade of a little learning. She believed that the unrest among women during the previous twenty years (1854–74) had been due to the Oxford movement, and warned men of the consequences of this religious revolt:

16. Dr Cullen to Mrs William Grey, 16 Nov. 1871 (Archives Public Day Schools Trust, Queen Anne's Gate, London).

The lords of creation may rest assured that if women are not devout ... they will soon cease to be practically obedient. There is no reason, except Divine Law, why women should be in subjection. Let men once succeed in shaking the faith of women in Divine Law (and remember that women will never rest satisfied with half-beliefs) and they will soon have friends to deal with like the women of the Commune.

She has a word of warning for women too:

... if ever the ideas of sexual equality take such root as to affect domestic rule, women may be sure that few sensible men will enter into a partnership for life on equal terms, an indissoluble union affecting the most intimate interests of life in which there is to be no authority to settle a difference of opinion, and no power of terminating a series of quarrels by dissolution of the bond.

She concluded by stating firmly that 'Woman's place is (with rare exceptions) in the home and her work is domestic'.

Convent schools reflected these views in their curricula. The subjects taken in the majority of convent boarding schools in the period 1838–78 included English, French, Italian, history, geography, use of the globes, writing, arithmetic, drawing, music, and needlework. Latin was not included in the programme of any of the French teaching orders of women (nuns), and mathematics was another subject which did not feature to any great extent in the advertisements of the period prior to 1880. The first examination results list of the Intermediate Education Board for Ireland, published in 1879, shows that the few girls' schools which did take Latin and mathematics were all Protestant schools, with the sole exception of one convent school, run by the Sisters of Mercy, Crumlin Road, Belfast, which included algebra. Out of 105 girls who passed mathematics (either Euclid or algebra or both) seventy-two, or sixty-eight per cent, were from Ulster.[17]

It was during Paul Cullen's period of office as archbishop of Dublin (1852–78) that the majority of French teaching orders of women were introduced into Ireland. These orders were: the Sacred Heart (1842), the Faithful Companions of Jesus (1844),

17. *Results List,* Intermediate Education Board, 1879.

St Louis (1859), St Joseph of Cluny (1860), and the Marists (1873).[18] They joined two other European teaching orders already at work in Ireland: the Dominicans (1644) and the Loreto order (1822) a branch of the Institute of the Blessed Virgim Mary. By the end of the nineteenth century sixty-two convent boarding schools had been established in Ireland. Out of the total only six were run by Irish religious orders (four Brigidine schools at Tullow, Mountrath, Abbeyleix, Goresbridge, one Mercy convent in Ennis, and one Holy Faith boarding school in Glasnevin, Dublin). This meant in effect that girls' secondary education in Ireland was dominated by religious orders whose educational views and traditions originated outside Ireland.

While orders such as the Ursulines, Sacred Heart, and the FCJ displayed the greatest degree of French influence, most convent boarding schools in Ireland were influenced to some degree by various aspects of French culture and traditions during the nineteenth century. Material supplied by a ninety-one-year-old Bridigine nun in 1937, giving an account of her school days in the early 1860s suggests that there was a strong emphasis on the French language at this time. The monthly examinations were called *matinées* and *soirées,* while there was a French governess employed in the school in 1855 so that both the nuns and the pupils could acquire the correct pronunciation in that language.[19] When advertising in the Catholic Directory for 1875, the Sacred Heart of Mary convent boarding school, Lisburn, Co. Antrim, also carefully emphasised the French language: 'As French is the language generally spoken in the convent, the pupils will have the advantage of learning to speak it fluently and with the purest accent.'

Mother Angela Kehoe's reminiscences of her school-days in the St Louis convent boarding school, Monaghan, in the 1860s, tells how French was the language of the school when she came in 1865.[20] Morning and night prayers were said in French and it was the custom to learn off by heart each Sunday the gospel of the day in French. The senior girls' classes were conducted almost entirely in French, the pupils soon becoming virtually bi-lingual. The French character of the school was highly

18. The Religious Orders and Congregations in Ireland (Dublin 1933). (Reprinted from *The Irish Jesuit Directory & Year Book,* 1933).
19. *Brigidine Centenary Record,* Tullow, 1937, p. 12.
20. Sister M. Pauline, *God Wills It* (Dublin 1959) p. 176.

approved of by parents, who saw in it an opportunity to give their daughters 'an advantage for which they would otherwise have had to go abroad'.

The printed programmes and prize lists for the period 1864–1900 for the Dominican convent boarding school in Cabra give some indication of the great emphasis placed on French culture, especially during the period 1871–81. French prizes were awarded regularly and in the school entertainment held after the annual distribution of prizes, there were songs, recitations, plays and operettas in French, for instance in 1878 Act III of Racine's *Esther,* in 1880 part of *Andromaque* and in 1881 *Marie Stuart* and Chant VII out of Voltaire's *Hendriade* formed part of the annual prizegiving ceremonies. The audience must have protested after this, as there appears to have been less emphasis on French plays.[21]

Another major feature of the French educational tradition, closely associated with the Jesuits, was the idea of emulation. All the evidence from Irish convent sources suggests that the majority of convent schools of French and European origin actively encouraged emulation by means such as frequent orals, written essays, an elaborate system of good conduct marks, repetitions and annual distribution of prizes. An advertisement from the Sacred Heart of Mary boarding and day school, Lisburn, Co. Antrim, in 1875, claimed that 'Emulation is encouraged by daily notes (marks), frequent competitions, marks of distinctions, quarterly recompenses (reports) and a general distribution of prizes at the end of the year.'[22]

Those who absented themselves frequently and for too long a time were reminded that they had no claim to these encouragements.

The emphasis placed by many Irish convents on politeness, deportment, good conduct, order, regularity, and application was another striking aspect of the French convent tradition in education at work in girls' schools in Ireland in the nineteenth century. In her account of the St Louis Order in Ireland, Sister Mary Pauline referred to Mother Genevieve Beale's insistence on the courtesies of life in their Monaghan school during the 1860s, the ritual of bowing, curtsying and saluting which had

21. Printed programme and prize lists 1864–1900. (Archives, Dominican Convent, Cabra).
22. *Catholic directory,* 1875.

formed part of the French convent tradition in education.[23] Kate O'Brien, in her semi-fictional account of her schooldays at the FCJ boarding school at Laurel Hill, Limerick, in the early twentieth century, considered that *la politesse* was a speciality on the FCJs. Education in this area was tackled thoroughly, especially with regard to table manners. On every Sunday evening marks were read out for Conduct (20), Silence (19), Politeness (20), Exactitude (10), Order (10) and Application (10). A mark lost for conduct was tantamount to expulsion: 'no one ever remembered it to have happened'.[24]

Finally the Jesuit aim of forming the judgment or developing what the French call *'le gout'* (good taste) was stressed in many Irish convent schools during the 19th century. The Ursuline Reglemens (Rules) for 1860 stressed that literature ought to develop 'a feeling for beauty, as well as love of truth and goodness'.[25] History was to be taught for its moral lessons: 'it ought to form the heart and the judgment'. The Sacred Heart Plan of Studies also stressed the great importance attached to the formation of judgment and and refinement of taste through various subjects, especially literature. In the First Class (highest) the class mistress was to encourage her pupils 'to write with a noble simplicity and to proportion the style to the subject ... this work ... will contribute above all to forming the judgment and the taste of these young people'.[26]

Mother Janet Erskine Stuart, a member of the Sacred Heart Order, writing in 1912, on the education of Catholic girls, showed her continuing adherence to these beliefs in her assertion that 'rational principles of aesthetics belong very intimately to the education of women'.[27] She considered that 'a girl's idea of beauty, her taste in art, will influence very powerfully her own life, and those of others ... if a women's taste is trained to choose the best, it upholds a standard which may save a whole generation from decadence'.

23. Sister M. Pauline, *op. cit.,* p. 131.
24. Kate O'Brien, *Land of Spices* (Reprinted Dublin, 1973) p. 72.
25. *Ursuline Reglemens,* 1860, p. 73 (Archives, Ursuline Convent, Thurles).
26. *Reglement des Pensionats et Plan d'Etudes de la Society du Sacre-Coeur de Jesus* (1887 edition), p. 110 (Archives, Sacred Heart Convent, Mount Anville, Dundrum).
27. M.J.E. Stuart, *The Education of Catholic Girls* (1912: Reprinted Maryland, 1964), p. 71.

It has been said of the Jesuits that in their eagerness to refine the taste of their pupils that they tended to present an idealized world from which all evil had been excluded, and this was a criticism which was later levelled at convent schools also. Mary Colum, writing about life in an Irish convent boarding school at the beginning of the twentieth century, run by a French order (St Louis, Monaghan) considered that education there, as in most of the convent schools of Europe, prior to the First World War, was out of touch with real life. 'Education was regarded as a means of fitting our souls for good rather than as a preparation for life'.[28] She was a pupil at three other convent schools in Europe, including Germany, and found that they all shared the same European Catholic tradition, which she termed 'aristrocratic'. Their standards of unselfishness, magnanimity, devotion to others she rarely found in the world afterwards.

One 'old convent-girl' writing in the 1870s about her school-days considered that convent boarding schools failed to prepare girls without any independent income to live alone in the world. There were, she found, usually two alternatives suggested to girls in convent schools: marry or become a nun. It was taken for granted that a girl would marry if she had no religious vocation.[29] Her final conclusion was that convent schools had played a vital role in educating the middle classes of Ireland during the period 1850–73. Proof of the refining influence of convent boarding schools could be found in the fact that these people of her generation were 'neat and their manners polite and quiet' and that they were generally honourable 'in pursuit of the only ambition which had as yet lighted up their mental horizon: that of making money'. She praised convent schools for the 'reading, writing, and piano playing, the refinement and ladylike manners and ideas, the self-respect and conscientiousness' which they had been spreading for the previous fifty years especially among the 'lower grade of the middle class'.

It appears that in the quest for social prestige through education Irish convent boarding schools supplied a certain status to their pupils which ensured the survival of these traditions until the mid-twentieth century: it is only in the last thirty years that

28. Mary Colum, *The Life and the Dream* (London, 1947) p. 31.
29. *Fraser's Magazine,* Oct. 1874, pp 473–83.

the majority of boarding schools have begun to decline.[30] The hallmark of this distinctive system of education was its emphasis on character formation, on discipline, on refinement and good taste, with particular emphasis on the French language and on literary style. This training received at such an impressionable age was to remain firmly engrained in adult life and provided their pupils with a counter element to the dominant anglicisation of their culture. This was an important element in the manners and lifestyle of a Catholic middle class which grew in influence in late nineteenth-century Ireland. The French orders in Ireland thus fulfilled the aims of the Catholic bishops who had accepted them in the 1840s and 1850s in the hope that they would provide an attractive alternative to the growing power of the state and of anglicisation.

While the French teaching orders did provide day schools for the elementary education of the poor, the majority of their second-level schools were boarding schools, catering mainly for the middle classes, with basic fees ranging from twenty to forty pounds per annun. As a result these schools acquired a certain status denied to the convent day schools of the Irish religious orders. Their role was seen at first as catering for the education of the poor and therefore with primary education. Nano Nagle started this trend by founding the Irish Presentation order (1775) to cater exclusively for the poor. This helps explain why the Presentation order established very few second-level schools in the nineteenth-century by comparison with the Mercy order, the largest of the five Irish religious orders dealing with the education of girls in Ireland. The other three were the Brigidines (1807), the Irish Sisters of Charity (1815), and the Holy Faith order (1866).

Class distinction and types of school

It was from two of these Irish orders that the only new initiative on girls' secondary education came from within Ireland during the nineteenth century. This was the idea of day-pension or 'pay' schools started by the Mercy and Presentation nuns. These schools, fifty-two in number, were an attempt to provide education for the Catholic middle and lower middle classes in the larger towns and cities of Ireland who could not afford to

30. Rev. J. A. Gilchrist, *The Irish Boarding School* in Hibernia, Christmas 1959.

send their daughters to convent boarding schools. The fees charged (two to four pounds per annum) were relatively low, and the majority of girls who attended these schools were the daughters of prosperous farmers and shopkeepers, who could afford to keep them at school until they were fifteen or sixteen years old.[31]

All the accounts of life in this period suggest that the class distinctions of society were the major factor in the growth of the convent pension school idea. The very title 'pension school', as distinct from the 'poor school', shows clearly that different schools were envisaged for the different social classes. Although there were variations in the titles used by the convent pension schools in the nineteenth century (select school, benefit school, private school) it is clear that they all aimed to retain the idea of an education for girls along class lines.

James Kavanagh, professor in the Catholic University (Stephen's Green), when questioned by the Powis Commission (a commission on primary education in the late 1860s) on the specific role of convent pension schools, claimed that they were 'Intermediate or middle class schools' and ranked 'above the primary while being below the regular convent boarding school.'[32] He considered that there was 'no real distinction in principle' between these day pension schools and the convent boarding schools. They were simply 'an acknowledgement of the social distinctions that existed in society'.

Although both the Mercy and Presentation orders were catering for much the same class of pupil as the Christian Brothers, they were not able to avoid this problem because of their acceptance of both the national school system and the pay school idea. Their efforts to cater for the middle classes in both their national and pay schools did lead to some confusion of aims, and greatly weakened the full development of their pension schools into secondary schools proper until the first decades of the twentieth century. The numbers in convent pension shools remained small (between thirty and fifty) until the early twentieth century, mainly because the convent national schools also attracted the growing middle classes. These two school systems operated parallel to each other, and sometimes

---

31. *Special Reports on Convent National Schools* in connection with the Board of National Education. H. C. 1864 (405) XLVI, pp 162–3.
32. *Powis Commission,* 1870, part iii, p. 446.

in competition with one another, for most of the nineteenth century. They were so closely intertwined that it is very difficult at times to separate the two. What can be said, though, is that the convent national schools and the convent pension schools of the Irish religious orders were two of the most important developments in the education of Catholic girls in the nineteenth century, because these were the only schools which gave them the opportunity to move upwards in society, catering as they did for both their primary and secondary education.

The changes brought about by the Intermediate examination system (1878–1910)

The introduction of the Intermediate Education (Ireland) Act of 1878 and the Royal University of Ireland Act of 1879 provided the real breakthrough in girls' secondary education in Ireland as they recognised for the first time the principle that girls and women had the right to sit for public competitive examinations and to take university degrees. The fact that public opinion in Ireland was at first generally against such examinations for girls, and that many girls did not have either the opportunity or the means to take immediate advantage of either of these Acts, does not alter their crucial importance as a force for changing the role of women in Irish society.

Under the Intermediate Eduction Act an Intermediate Board of Education was set up to hold annual competitive examinations, on the results of which prizes and exhibitions (£20 Junior Grade, £30 Middle Grade and £50 Senior Grade) were awarded to pupils and 'results fees' to schools (payments on each subject passed by a student). It was in the area of examinations that this Act was to make its most decisive contribution to girls' secondary education, insisting on certain age limits (under sixteen for Junior Grade, under seventeen for Middle Grade, and under eighteen years for Senior Grade examinations), widening the range of subjects and in the process giving it a structure which it had not possessed before. National schools were excluded from results fees and as a result convent national schools began to assume their proper role as feeders to convent pension schools. In many cases the junior section of convent pension schools now became detached from the senior part, and either remained as private junior schools or else were amalgamated with the convent national schools.

While in theory students could select any number of subjects

44

so long as they included two of the following, Latin, Greek, English, mathematics and modern languages, in practice certain subjects were given much higher marks than others. Thus English, Greek and Latin were worth 1200 marks, while German and French had only 700 marks and Celtic trailed behind with 600 marks. As the valuable exhibitions were awarded on the total aggregate of marks gained, there was a strong inducement to schools to teach Latin and mathematics, and to present a student with ability in as many subjects as possible. The money prizes went direct to the students while the schools gained results fees only on each subject passed. However the prestige attached to winning such valuable exhibitions was considerable. The newspapers started publishing the names of the various schools, listing them in order of the total number of exhibitions and prizes won. This ceated a growing competition between schools and gradually most convent schools were drawn into the fray.

Catholic/Protestant academic rivalry

Apart from the Intermediate examination system, the other great force for change in the education of girls was the establishment of the Royal University of Ireland, which opened university examinations to women for the first time. The RUI was an examining body only, and did not offer instruction, and since women were debarred from the male universities, they had to seek a university-type education elsewhere that would prepare them for the RUI examinations.

In 1885, Dr William Walsh was appointed Catholic archbishop of Dublin. He realised that the Intermediate and RUI examinations were becoming more and more the arbiters of a school's excellence as far as public opinion was concerned. It was made clear to Dr Walsh shortly after his appointment, by Sister Hanley of the Dominican convent in Eccles Street (Dublin), that if the bishops wished to retain control of the education of women, they would have to take the new situation into account. Sister Hanley had been eagerly awaiting Dr Walsh's appointment, as she wished to start university classes in Eccles Street. She reminded him that Eccles Street had been founded in 1883 primarily as an alternative to Alexandra College for Catholic girls.[33] Sister Hanley now suggested that if

33. D.D.A. Walsh Papers 1885. Sr A. Hanley to Dr Walsh, 24 June 1885.

the nuns did not provide university education for their past pupils both from the Sion Hill and the Eccles Street schools then the girls would go on to the Protestant Alexandra.

It seems unlikely that Dr Walsh would have made any moves in the direction of girls' university education in the 1880s had it not been for the threat posed by the collegiate courses of Alexandra College. He seems to have been loath to make any hasty changes in this direction when the whole question of Catholic university education was still unresolved. It appears from his correspondence with Sister Hanley that, under the stimulus of the Intermediate and RUI examinations, parents of girls in convent schools were now demanding a collegiate or university-type education for their daughters. Dr Walsh accepted this situation and university classes were quickly established in Eccles Street in September 1885. These were continued until 1893, when St Mary's University College was founded at Merrion Square, Dublin. Because of its university work, the curriculum of the Eccles Street secondary school included Latin and mathematics, in addition to the usual convent subjects, English, French, German, arithmetic, book-keeping, piano, drawing and religious knowledge. The inclusion of Latin and mathematics was vital to the convent schools who hoped to compete effectively for exhibitions and prizes in the Intermediate examinations with Protestant girls schools, and this message was not lost on the bishops.

The *Freeman's Journal,* dealing with the Intermediate results for 1887, noted that, while in the teaching of modern languages the convent schools had reasserted their superiority, they were completely outpaced by their Protestant rivals because of their lack of mathematics. The editorial accepted that in most convent schools it was impossible to give greater attention to mathematics, as their system of teaching was not geared to it, but urged convent schools where possible to readjust their system of teaching to suit the requirements of the Intermediate system. The Catholic bishops now began to respond to the growing volume of public opinion on the need for change. In Cork city a new day convent school of the Ursuline order was established in August 1887 by the bishop of Cork, Dr. O'Callaghan.

The new day school was called St Angela's High School for Girls, which suggests that it was to be animated by the same emphasis on higher education as the English high schools for girls.[34] The inclusion of mathematics and Latin in the first prospectus of St Angela's indicates the same approach to girls' secondary education as the high school movement. The basic course of studies included religious education, history, English, geography, natural philosophy, domestic economy, and the fee was four pounds *per annum* for girls over twelve years. Extras were mathematics, Latin, German, Italian, drawing, piano, singing, violin and guitar.

There was a tremendous demand for such a day school: within a month of the opening of St Angela's (September 1887), there were 260 pupils present and forty disappointed parents had to be turned away.

This significant departure from the traditional type of convent boarding schools was justified within a year (1888) when Mary Ryan, one of its pupils, gained first place in Ireland in the Junior Grade examinations with a total of twelve subjects: English, French, arithmetic, drawing, music, domestic economy, Latin, Euclid, algebra, natural philosophy, botany and book-keeping.[35] She went on to repeat this success in Middle Grade in 1890, taking second place in Senior Grade in 1891. The logical outcome of this approach to education was the opening of university classes at St Angela's to prepare for the RUI examinations, and this was duly authorised by the bishop in 1890.

The Loreto order also established university classes in St. Stephen's Green at this time, conducted side by side with their Intermediate classes. The effect on their secondary school can be judged from the results list of the Intermediate Board for 1896, when three out of the four St Stephen's Green pupils who entered for Senior Grade won exhibitions. One student won a gold medal for first place in Ireland in classics, another a prize for Latin and for Italian composition. The roll book for the period 1893–1903 shows that the classes in the secondary school were now organised on the basis of the Intermediate examinations: seventh class (highest) was Senior Grade, sixth was Middle Grade, fifth Junior Grade and fourth was Preparatory Grade.

Archbishop Walsh of Dublin made it clear in a speech in 1894 that the battle for supremacy in the examination stakes was

---

34. *Printed Prospectus, Ursuline Day School, St Angela's, Cork.*
35. *Results List,* Intermediate Education Board, 1888.

now only starting for convent schools.[36] He was aware that both Alexandra College and School and the Ladies' Collegiate School, Belfast, who were among the most consistent contenders for first place in the overall list of distinctions in the Intermediate examinations, were greatly helped by their university work, which ensured a higher standard because of the highly qualified staff of lecturers and teachers necessary for this work, and because of the number of able girls attracted to such institutions on account of the special facilities offered. Thus the first tentative links between girls' higher and Intermediate education was being forged in the 1890s by this desire to defeat the Protestant girls' schools and colleges in the Intermediate prize lists.

It is significant that the first marked increase in the number of convent schools participating in the Intermediate examinations took place in 1893, coinciding with the establishment of St Mary's University College by Dr Walsh. There were twenty-nine convent schools featured on the results lists in 1893, an increase of nine on the previous year. Gradually their numbers increased until by 1898 there were forty-five convent schools on the Intermediate results lists. It appears from all the available sources that convent schools were being actively encouraged to take these examinations in the 1890s. In 1893 the Ursulines in Sligo were advised by Fr Clancy, a professor in Maynooth College and later Bishop of Elphin, to prepare pupils for the Intermediate examinations.[37] By 1895 the Ursulines in Sligo and Waterford were both participating in these examinations, while by 1897 the Dominicans in Galway had also entered the competitive lists, acting on the advice of their new provincial, Dr Hickey.

A typescript by a St Louis nun, Sister Laurentia Stuart, who had started as a boarder at St Louis Convent, Monaghan, in September 1897, aged thirteen years, suggests that the main emphasis at this time was on beating the Protestant schools in the Intermediate examinations: it was put to the pupils that they should aim at replacing Protestant supremacy in the exhibitions lists.[38] Born in 1884, near Killaloe, Co Clare, one of a family of sixteen children, she had been sent to the Monaghan

36. *Printed Annals of Sion Hill,* 3 May, 1894, p. 206.
37. *Ursuline Centenary Annual,* Sligo, 1850–1950, p. 21.
38. Typescript of Sr M. Laurentia Stuart (St Louis Convent, Rathmines) (now deceased).

convent because her father, a farmer, had been advised by the local parish priest that it was the leading convent school in the Intermediate examinations. She remembers that the Middle and Senior Grade students got up 'voluntarily' around 5am for months before the examination. Sister M. Raphael would appear around 6am with a plate of bread and jam for the students. Sister Laurentia took eleven subjects in Middle Grade: Celtic, English, French, German, Italian, commercial French, history, geography, mathematics, theory of music and theory of domestic science. For the first time in November 1896, a professor at the diocesan seminary came to the convent once a week (one and a half to two hours on Monday evening) to teach extra mathematics to the Intermediate Middle Grade pupils. Likewise in December 1896, Dr Mulhern, president of the diocesan seminary, came to give lessons in Latin to the Middle Grade students on a once-a-week basis.

The results of this intensification of effort was made manifest in 1899 when St Louis, Monaghan, achieved its greatest triumph, being just beaten into second place overall by Victoria College, Belfast (Mrs Byers Ladies' Collegiate School). The measure of this achievement can only be understood by comparing the number of pupils in each school and the number who entered for the Intermediate examinations. Mrs Byers admitted before the Intermediate Education Commission in 1899 that out of a total of 190 students in Victoria College, only 100 to 110 were in the Intermediate classes, and sixty-one of these passed in 1898. The corresponding figure for Monaghan was much smaller: there were only forty boarders in November 1897, and thirty-eight pupils were presented in the Intermediate examinations of 1898. All passed and eight gained exhibitions.

However, it was not until 1901 that the first convent school finally succeeded in defeating its Protestant rivals. Significantly, it was one which had been associated with university work almost from its inception: Dominican Convent, Eccles Street. It gained first in the overall list with thirty-nine distinctions, with Victoria High School, Derry (Miss McKillip's School) in second place (thirty-four), and Alexandra College and School sharing third place with Victoria College, Belfast (twenty-nine distinctions).

Another sign of the changing situation in the convent schools was the winning of the mathematics medal in both the

Middle and Junior Grade by St Mary's University College, Dublin, and Dominican Convent, Eccles Street, respectively, in 1900. These mathematics medals for first place in Ireland in this subject, had long been looked on as 'the property of Ulster Protestant schools' according to the *Weekly Freeman*.

From a position where only twenty convent schools featured on the results list of the Intermediate Board in 1892, to forty-five by 1898, and to first overall school in the prizewinners' list of 1901, the growth and change in direction of Catholic girls' education in Ireland was fundamental in nature. Even if forced on a less than wholehearted church establishment by lay parental pressure, by 1900 Catholic girls in Ireland were educationally poised to enter the new century on more equal terms with boys than could reasonably have seemed possible twenty years earlier.

Education for employment

Because Irish parents were determined that their daughters should gain their share of economic rewards, aristocratic ideals as laid down by the French convent tradition (the concept of a gentlewomen and all that it implied, the accomplishments, *la politesse* and marriage as the only alternative to the convent) were an anachronism by the beginning of the twentieth century in the race for prizes and material progress. A permanent pensionable career was becoming an acceptable role for a Catholic woman, and it was this development which was the decisive factor in the general acceptance of the Intermediate system for girls.

The career opportunities opening up to Irish girls in the period 1880–1910 also gave them and their parents a continuing impetus to strive for a recognised educational level and thereby ensured the full acceptance of the competitive examination system.

Factors which helped in this process were the opening up of the post office examinations to girls on a competitive basis; the desire of employers to gain cheap clerical labour; the high percentage of unmarried women in Ireland; and improved educational standards for girls.

The post office was the official pioneer of women's employment in both England and Ireland during the last two decades of the nineteenth century.[39] It was the only government depart-

39. *The Civil Service Competitor* (London) 28 Aug. 1903.

ment employing female clerical labour on a large scale. The reason appears to have been mainly economic, as the pay it fixed for women was considerably less than that for men.[40] In fact this caused some outcry in England at the time, as it was prophesied that women, by working for less money, would decrease the chances of male employment in the civil service and would lower its status as a job.[41]

In spite of these gloomy prognostications, the civil service opened up the first real opportunities for girls of ability to obtain clerical jobs on a purely competitive basis. As early as 1871 it had started examinations for female telegraph learners aged fifteen to eighteen years, while the first competitive examination for female clerks in the London post office took place in 1881.[42] In the case of the latter, seventy-six girls were selected out of the 747 who passed the first qualifying test. The age limit for female clerks was eighteen to twenty years, the subjects taken were arithmetic, English composition, geography and English history, and the salary offered, £55 *per annum*, rising to £80 *per annum* made it one of the best paid of the civil service jobs open to women. By February 1882 a National Schools inspector in Ireland was already noting the stimulating effect this was having on some National Schools pupils who were now 'beginning to be influenced by the ambitious desire to obtain places in the civil service — even the females have competed for PO appointments'.[43] He stated that two candidates from Co Wexford had obtained second and third place in Ireland, and seventeenth and eighteenth place overall in the UK at recent post office examinations. Both of these girls had been monitresses — one in the Presentation convent, Enniscorthy, the other in a school in the north of Ireland. Qualifying examinations for female sorters (fifteen to eighteen years) were being held at this stage, in reading and copying manuscript, handwriting, spelling, arithmetic and geography of the UK, although the first competitive examinations for these did not take place until 1894.[44]

40. *The Fingerpost: A Guide to Professions for Educated Women* (issued by the Central Bureau for the Environment of Women) London, 1906, p. 198.
41. *Clark's Civil Service Weekly,* iii and iv, 1901–2, p. 26.
42. *F.J.,* 29 Aug. 1882.
43. *48th Report of the Commissioners of National Education in Ireland,* 1881. H.C. 1882/c.3243/xxiv, p. 85.
44. *The Weekly Nation,* 28 Oct. 1899.

In the 1890s 'lady typewriters', as they were called at first, were increasingly being employed in the larger departments of the English civil service, although these appointments were not made by open competition until 1899. The first civil service typist appointed in Ireland was in 1901, in the Department of Agriculture and Technical Instruction.

The civil service directory for 1889 indicates that the only appointments made to the G.P.O. sorting office in Dublin at that time were telegraphists: nineteen first-class telegraphists earned from twenty-seven to thirty-two shillings a week while fifty second-class telegraphists were paid from ten to twenty-six shillings, and there were three female supervisors at annual salaries of £85 to £105. Oral evidence from a past pupil of the Dominican convent, Eccles Street, suggests that even during the second decade of the twentieth century most women and girl clerks were still being appointed first to England, and immediately put their name down for transfer to Ireland, whenever such an appointment might arise.[45]

The introduction of a language (French or German) in addition to English, history, geography, and arithmetic for the women clerks examination and the new class of girl clerks in 1897 considerably altered these examinations, as the extra 400 marks for a language gave Intermediate girls an immediate advantage over other candidates for these appointments. Delia O'Dwyer, who obtained the first Irish place at the examination for women clerks in March 1898, had completed her Inter-mediate course at the Dominican convent, Eccles Street, while another past pupil of the same convent gained sixth place in the UK in the same examination in 1899.[46] Both girls had joined the classes of the Civil Service Institute, 31 Rutland Square, and their successes were used by that Institute as proof that 'under the present system Intermediate girls should almost monopolise the Irish successes at the Women and Girl Clerks examinations'.

The competitive aspects of the civil service examinations were particularly important at a time when the class distinctions of society tended to limit middle-class women to narrow occupational spheres. Respectability more than anything else often determined the choice of future career for many middle-

45. Information supplied by Mrs M. O'Flaherty, 29 Mobhi Road, Dublin 9.
46. *The Weekly Nation*, 9 Sept. 1899.

class women. Bishop O'Dwyer of Limerick, reviewing a book on women's work in 1895, used the occasion to launch a bitter tirade against the appalling working and living conditions of many shop assistants, who suffered long hours, often hideous ventilation, bad sanitation, wretched 'living-in' accommodation, poor food and the possibility of unconditional dismissal because the conventions of society dictated that such jobs carried with them the precious aura of respectabiity.[47]

Bishop O'Dwyer considered that most of these abuses could have been redressed more easily had the girls not been 'cursed with respectability' which left them vulnerable and helpless to mitigate the evils under which they suffered. Even as late as 1904 when the Irish Central Bureau for the Employment of Women was listing the jobs available to women on its books, it referred to lady servants, lady dairy workers, lady gardeners, lady helps, and lady laundresses.[48] While the civil service examinations widened the job opportunities for girls in Ireland, it was those living in the larger urban areas, such as Belfast, Cork and Dublin, who were particularly well placed to take advantage of these examinations. These were the three centres for the civil service examinations for girls in Ireland and, as a result, special coaching establishments were set up to prepare girls for these examinations in those cities.[49]

The census returns for 1911 underlined the importance of employment for many women in Ireland. There was a high percentage of unmarried women aged fifteen years and upwards (48.26 per cent) in the population,[50] and for many women employment on some kind of permanent basis was not just a matter of choice, but a necessity.

New employment opportunities for women

Gradually in the opening decade of the twentieth century new job opportunities were opened up for girls with secretarial training. The first examinations for four lady clerkships was held by Guinness's brewery in June 1906,[51] while twenty-three

47. *New Ireland Review,* iii, No. 5, July 1895, p. 311.
48. *Irish Central Bureau for the Employment of Women,* Dublin (1905), p. 26 Reports 1904–5.
49. *The General Advertiser,* 1 Jan. 1898.
50. *General Report of the Census of Ireland,* 1911. H.C. 1912–13, CXVIII, p. xxvi.
51. *The Civil Servcie Competitor,* 4 Jan, 1907.

posts in various Dublin offices were obtained by pupils of Skerry's School of Shorthand and Typewriting by December 1906. This slow beginning heralded the dawn of a new era which offered ever-increasing employment opportunities for women in office work. The census returns for 1911 show the tremendous increase in the number of women employed as commercial clerks during the period 1891–1911. While there were only 907 women clerks in 1891, they numbered 3437 by 1901 and 7849 (including female typists) in 1911.[52]

Conclusion

The period 1860–1910 was a time of transition in Irish society as a whole. The reality of power was for the first time passing to a group in Ireland, the middle class, who were part of the majority religious group in the island. The mainspring of all this change was education, and in particular the public competitive examination system of the period 1880–1910, which was seen as the passport to status and privilege and power. Middle-class girls shared in this transfer of power: at the beginning of this period the provision of secondary education for girls of the middle class was in itself a revolutionary concept. Yet by the beginning of the twentieth century not only had this idea been accepted, but also that of the higher education of girls, while a whole new range of career opportunities were beginning to be opened up to them.

From these small beginnings in England and Ireland and in other European and North American countries, the changes in the employment prospects for women brought about by the industrial revolution has had an important bearing on the growth and expansion of education opportunities for women. In historical terms, this opening up of opportunities for independence and personal development for women across great areas of economic activity is one of the major social movements of the twentieth century. The women's movement, as it has come to be called, has had and is still having a profound effect on how we as women see ourselves and organise ourselves.

52. General Report of the Census of Ireland, 1911, p. xxviii.

Charting New Waters: women's experience in higher eduction, 1879–1908[1]

EIBHLÍN BREATHNACH

In 1873 Isabella Tod, feminist, suffragist and founder of the Belfast Ladies' Institute, first expressed the demand for women's higher education.[2] The occasion was the introduction by Gladstone of a University Bill for Ireland which proposed to amalgamate the two existing Protestant universities in the country, Queen's University (which had three constituent Queen's Colleges in Belfast, Cork and Galway) and Dublin University (Trinity College). Addressing a meeting of the Queen's Institute, an institution which provided technical instruction and training for women, in Dublin, Isabella Tod expressed the fear that if women could find no place in the bill, they could be excluded from the benefits of higher education for a further fifty years. In the event, the bill failed to pass, but Tod's challenge provoked the Queen's Institute to appeal to Trinity College to extend its educational privileges to women. The board of the college, however, refused the request on the grounds 'that they do not think it desirable that the education of young men and young women should be conducted in the manner proposed, which appears to involve very serious practical difficulties'.[3] A similar request by the Belfast Ladies' Institute to Queen's University also met with a refusal. Yet, when the motion approving the admission of women to university degrees was debated in convocation (the forum for graduates of the university to express their opinions) it was defeated by the slimmest of margins: sixteen votes to fifteen.

---

1. This paper is based on research done for an MA thesis 'Women and Higher Education in Ireland 1860–1912', (UCD 1981); the extended and revised thesis will be published in full in 1988.
2. *Journal of Women's Education Union*, i, no. 4 (15 April 1873) p. 72.
3. J. Carson, Registrar, Board of Trinity College to A. B. Corlett, Secretary of Queen's Institute of Female Professional Schools for Improving the Education of Women, reply to memorial, 18 Oct 1873 (TCD ms 2154).

The position of women in society and in education

In retrospect, these demands for higher education for women seem to have been somewhat premature. The developments in female education during the 1850s and 1860s were not uniformly directed towards seeking the admission of women to university. The belief that the ideal model for girls' education was one where systemic learning was tested and certified by a recognised body was shared only by the more advanced members of Protestant educational circles. The prospectus of (the Protestant) Alexandra College in 1866 stated that the aims of the college were 'to afford an education more sound and solid, more systematically imparted and better tested than is at present easily to be obtained by women of the middle and upper classes in this country'. Margaret Byers, founder of Victoria College in Belfast in 1859 expressed the same belief in her often expressed desire 'to afford girls the same opportunities for sound scholarship that was given to their brothers in the best boys' schools'.[5] But for the majority of schools run by Catholic religious orders the purpose of education was expressed in more lofty terms. Madame Barat, founder of the Faithful Companions of Jesus, believed that the ideal end-product of middle-class secondary education was a 'truly Christian wife and mother of a family who is solidly virtuous and attached by religion to all her duties'. The writer Mary Colum, wrote that education in the St Louis Convent, Monaghan, was 'regarded as a means of fitting our souls for good rather than as a preparation for life'.[6]

The role of women in nineteenth-century Ireland was incompatible with the widespread acceptance of the need for women's higher education. The notion of women's role and nature prevalent at the time was derived from two influences, one rooted in the Catholic devotion to Our Lady, virgin and mother which also encompassed the polar opposite figure of Eve. The other was drawn from the Victorian ideal of service and devotion to men, personified by the sombre persona of

---

4. Moody and Beckett, *Queen's Belfast 1845–1949, The History of a University* (Faber and Faber, London 1959) i, 321.
5. *Third Report of the Commissioners on University Education in Ireland,* [c.1229] H.C., 1902 xxxii.
6. Mary Colum, *The Life and the Dream,* (Doubleday and Co. New York 1947).

Victoria herself.[7] Marriage and child-bearing were considered the ends for which women were created. Only in the Catholic tradition was there an alternative (considered indeed worthier), that of entering a convent. Within the bonds of marriage the daily existence of women was determined by class. Notions of respectability, as inflexible as any law, cemented the class division. The lifestyle considered appropriate to each rank in society was not just absorbed but consciously passed on from one generation to the next. Women were both victims and perpetrators of the multiplicity of social rules which governed and restricted their behaviour. At the lower end of the social spectrum, where economic necessity gave women an independence unknown to their middle-class sisters, the restrictions were less. While it was common and accepted that lower-class women would work both in and out of the home, the mores of middle-class society saw women as excluded rigidly from work outside the home. Only those left destitute were permitted to work, and even then they were limited to teaching or sewing. Their education ensured that they were fit for little else, if even that, so completing the vicious circle.

It was the plight of middle-class women who found themselves penniless as a result of the death or profligacy of their husbands or fathers which had sparked off the movement to improve middle-class female education both in England and Ireland. The problems, which were more acute in England with its large middle class, were taken up by those of a liberal bent who sought educational reform along with other reforms, such as the right of married women to control their own property.[8] The Irish movement originated in the same circles, among the Protestant urban middle class, many of whom were known to have Liberal sympathies. Whereas the English movement gradually won acceptance for its educational goals within the House of Commons, this was not the case in Ireland where the emergence of the women's movement coincided with the death of Irish Liberalism. This forced the Irish movement to seek allies in England. This paid off. The inclusion of girls in the Intermediate Act 1878 (which provided for public examina-

7. See, M. MacCurtain, 'Toward an Appraisal of the Religious Image of Women', in *The Crane Bag,* iv, no. 1. (1980) pp 26–30.
8. J. Kamm, *Hope Deferred, Girls' Education in English History* (Mathuem, London 1965).

tions for second-level students) was the result of the success of a delegation organised by the indefatigable Isabella Tod in winning support of both government and opposition.[9] However, Isaac Butt, leader of the Home Rule party did not share this enthusiasm. He sourly commented that 'the cry for Intermediate education in Ireland had no reference whatsoever to girls'.[10]

In 1879 a new University Bill for Ireland was announced. This proposed to dissolve the Protestant Queen's University and to replace it with a new non-denominational Royal University of Ireland. The RUI was to be purely an examining body; it would not offer instruction (though it would appoint teaching fellows), and it would be up to the students to study at any college they chose, or privately, in order to prepare themselves for the RUI examinations. On the announcement of the bill, Isabella Tod, helped by Courtney, Liberal member for Liskeard, established an *ad hoc* committee whose object was to ensure the admission of women to degrees in the RUI.

The response to the new opportunities now unexpectedly opened to women was very muted. The demand for access to degrees was made only by that small band of educationalists in Belfast and Dublin. They found no support among the population at large. The path of the first students was made difficult by the fact that though they had a right to sit examinations and be awarded degrees, no specific arrangements had been made for their actual education. This strange anomaly arose because the Royal University was only an examining board.[12] The twenty-eight fellows who served as university examiners were obliged to teach but the senate had assigned them to the existing male colleges. The first nine women who graduated in 1884 had solved the problem of teaching in various ways. Four attended classes in both Alexandra College and McIntosh and Tinkler, a grind establishment. Louise McIntosh took all her classes in her brother's grinder, Alice Oldham combined classes in Alexandra College with some in the Royal College of Surgeons, and the remaining two attended classes in Alexandra and in Rutland School in Mountjoy Square.[13]

9. Hansard 3, ccxli, 416 (28 June 1878).
10. *Ibid,* 1817 (12 Aug 1878).
11. J.W.E.U., ix, no. 99 (15 Mar 1881), p. 38.
12. 42 & 43 Vict., ch. 65.
13. Minutes of the Senate of the Royal University of Ireland (Thom., Dublin 1887) i, 240–2.

Their graduation attracted considerable interest. Mary Hayden, then a second-year student, recorded the occasion in her diary:[14]

the long procession of hooded and gowned male graduates, all the girls coming last. As soon as they appeared at the door, there was a burst of applause. They looked exceedingly well in their black gowns, hoods lined with white fur and tasselled caps, even the plain ones and the ordinary ones appeared to advantage ... Charlotte Taylor went up to the organ, sat down on the bench with her silk blue hood hanging gracefully down behind her, played the piece which was her 'thesis' for the B.Mus degree, accompanied by a full orchestra of about 100 people. There was a great deal of applause. Then the Duke (of Abercorn) arose and made a rather long speech, he referred to the girls at some length and quoted that hackneyed old line about "sweet girl graduates" whereat Henry McIntosh was convulsed with laughter. The girls walked up with great dignity and composure amidst loud applause and the five honours B.A.'s separately, the four pass together. Jessie Twemlow, Marion Kelly, Miss Sands and the Chief (Isabella Mulvany) looked especially well; not a bit the typical blue stocking which I was glad to see, since Chief Justice Morris, having only seen Alice Oldham, pronounced them 'an ugly lot'.[14]

The *ad hoc* nature of the arrangements made by women students for teaching were in sharp contrast to the facilities available to their male counterparts. The Belfast Ladies' Institute was first to seek a solution. In September 1882 they requested Queen's College, Belfast, that women be admitted to honours classes. The council agreed and the first women to attend went to lectures in Greek, mathematics and experimental physics.[15] Seven year later in 1889 women were admitted to the medical classes. Despite the early availability of lectures in Queen's College, Victoria College found itself faced with demands to start university classes for aspiring graduates. After some initial hesitation on the part of the staff, Margaret Byers set up a separate university department and by 1888 twelve students had graduated in arts. Other northern

14. Diary of Mary Hayden, 22 Oct 1884 (NLI ms 16,641).
15. Council minutes of Queen's College, Belfast, 21 Oct 1882 p. 282 (QCB f 824).

schools followed suit, Intermediate School in Newry, Endowed School in Banger, Methodist College, Belfast, Ladies' Collegiate School in Derry and others.

Queen's College Cork was next to open its doors, and in 1886 five women entered the college.[16] It was remarked the following year that their presence 'greatly contributed to the preservation of order' and it was expected that 'their example will stimulate the men to more attentive and regular work'; but alas, it was not reported whether this lofty expectation was fulfilled.[17] Queen's College Galway admitted women in 1888 but the local Catholic bishop, F. J. McCormack, took exception and issued a declaration which was read in all the Catholic churches in the dioceses, forbidding Catholic girls to attend.[18] All in all, fourteen institutions, including the three Queen's Colleges, offered teaching to degree level to women students during the first ten years of the Royal University. During that period 753 women passed examinations in arts and of that number 291 studied in one of the colleges. In addition to these fourteen colleges, there was a much larger number of schools and colleges which prepared students for first arts and even second arts examinations and an even larger number of schools entered girls for the matriculation examination.

Ironically, Dublin students found the greatest difficulties in finding university-level teaching. Even the authorities of Alexandra, who had been very quick to organise university classes, felt that their students were at a disadvantage because all the fellows, who were also the university examiners, assigned to Dublin were concentrated in University College which was run by the Jesuits and where Catholic men studied for RUI examinations. Female Catholic students had the additional complaint that the only teaching available to them was in the Protestant Alexandra. Dr Delany, SJ, who had been appointed president of University College, had very conservative views on the subject of women's education and was opposed to male and female students being educated together. When he was approached in 1882 by women undergraduates for permission to attend the fellows' lectures he refused their

16. *Report of the President of Queen's College, Cork for the session 1886–7,* 7, [c.5203] H.C. 1887, xii, 851.
17. *Ibid.,* for 1887–8, 1888 [c.5484] xl, 45.
18. *Report of the President of Queen's College Galway for the session 1887–8,* 7, [c.5437] H.C. 1888 xl, 79.

request.[19] Aggrieved, they took their case to the senate of the university, and in a 'memorial' (petition) pointed out the disadvantages of not being able to attend the fellows' lectures. The senate adopted a cautious line and in their reply regretted their inability to interfere with the private arrangements of the institutions where the fellows gave their lectures. In recognition of the genuineness of their case, they offered rooms in Earlsfort Terrace to any fellow from University College who was willing to repeat his lectures to women students.[20]

Some fellows, notably Fr Finlay, offered their service to the women undergraduates. Mary Hayden recorded in her diary her attendance at philosophy lectures given by Fr Finlay and French lectures conducted by the Abbé Polin. In his case, discretion proved the better part of valour. She observed,[21] 'this day was only notable by reason of the introduction of Mrs Hayes into the Abbé's French class in the capacity of matron, which considering the age, appearance and profession of the teacher and pupils seemed a little unnecessary'. The arrangement did not last longer than two to three years; some fellows disliked repeating their lectures while others charged fees beyond the reach of the women students, most of whom were already paying fees to Alexandra.

In 1888 Margaret Downes, a second-year student who had moved from Cork where she had attended the Queen's College, became incensed by the unavailability of similar facilities in Dublin. So she organised a new petition among the Catholic graduates and undergraduates, who were, she felt, particularly discriminated against. The senate stuck to its original decision while repeating its expressions of sympathy at the plight of the women students. Unappeased, Margaret Downes took to print and in a pamphlet entitled *The Case of the Catholic Lady Student of the Royal University* she argued that the senate's refusal to redress the women students' grievances falsified the 'liberal professions of the founders of the University'.[22] Thus the purpose for which the university was founded, the satisfac-

19. Fr Lambert McKenna, Fr William Delany and his work for Irish Education (unpublished ms in Jesuit Archives, Leeson Street, Dublin) pp. 197, 248, 289.
20. RUI sen min., 1, 119.
21. Mary Hayden diary, 12 Nov 1883 (NLI ms 16,638).
22. Margaret M. Downes, *The Case of the Catholic Lady Students of the Royal University Stated,* (Dublin 1888).

tion of Catholic claims for higher education, was frustrated. Her passionate outpourings, however, attracted little support; the number of women were too few and Catholic attitudes too conservative to force the senate to impose women students on the authorities of University College. Left to fend for themselves, the majority of Catholic women undergraduates attended Alexandra Collge, its Protestant atmosphere notwithstanding.

Demands for change

The sudden changes in female education brought about by the Intermediate Act and the Royal University created a need for some group which would seek to protect the new opportunities given to women in the uncertain and often hostile climate into which they were launched. A nucleus of such a group existed in Belfast around Victoria College and the Belfast Ladies' Institute and in Dublin around Alexandra College and the Queen's Institute. The first group was formed in Belfast shortly after the Intermediate Act was passed. The Belfast Ladies' Institute had united with school-teachers in liaison with professors from Queen's College to form the Ulster Schoolmistresses' Association in 1881.

A similar move took place in Dublin in 1882. At a meeting in the provost's house in Trinity, which was attended by members of the staff of Alexandra College and the governing committee of the Queen's Institute, Louisa Digges La Touche, headmistress of Alexandra College, moved that an association be formed with the object of promoting higher education for women in Ireland. They charged themselves with the tasks of acting as a medium of communication between schoolteachers and other ladies interested in education and of watching over the interests of girls especially with regard to Intermediate education and the Royal University.

The Dublin association took on the role of the central body, calling itself the Central Association of Schoolmistresses and other Ladies Interested in Education (CAISM) and the Ulster group served as a branch, though on the strict understanding that no general statement of policy would be issued without prior agreement.[23] In 1888 a branch in Cork was set up and

23. Minutes of the Central Association of Irish Schoolmistresses and other Ladies interested in Education, 2 May 1882 (in care of Miss M. Jago, Blackrock).

both Galway and Derry had a corresponding member. The leading figure of the new association was its secretary Alice Oldham. She had been a member of the delegation from Ireland seeking the inclusion of girls in the Intermediate Act and was among the first nine women graduates of the Royal University. Coming from a well-known merchant family, she was noted, along with the other females of her family, for her 'long nose and iron will'.[24] The latter quality served the CAISM to good advantage. She was tireless in her devotion to her new duties and the success which attended the CAISM's efforts to promote the cause of women in education was in no small measure due to her unflagging commitment.

The toughest campaign embarked on by the association was their attempt to persuade the board of Trinity College to admit women to its degrees and lectures. The appointment of Dr Salmon as Provost in 1888 ushered in an era where women's claims for admission were thwarted at every turn by a board dominated by the conservative ideas of its new provost. The attraction of a Trinity degree over that conferred by the Royal University was considerable. The status accorded to its degrees was higher and its Church of Ireland ethos was more acceptable to Dublin Protestants than was the non-denominational RUI. There were even weightier considerations. The success of the Liberal party in 1892 with its commitment to Home Rule seemed to threaten the existing university institutions. A reconstituted university such as might be expected from the planned Home Rule parliament could demand college attendance as part of its degree requirements. This threatened the existing arrangements for university classes and faced Protestant students, in the event of Trinity's failure to admit them as students, with the unwelcome alternative of attending the Jesuit University College in order to acquire a degree.

The CAISM chose the occasion of the college's tercenterary to make its demand.[25] Four memorials seeking the admission of women were sent to the board as preliminaries in a campaign which was to a very large extent organised by Alice Oldham. The reaction of the board, tersely recorded in the minutes was

24. Family information from niece, Miss Edith Woodward.
25. There is a good account of this in W. G. Brooke (ed.) *Proceedings of Movement for the Admission of Women to Trinity College Dublin* (Dublin 1895).

that 'it was not prepared to effect these changes'.[26] Presumably in order to avoid any hint of dissension during the tercentenary celebrations, the message to the CAISM was that consideration of their request had to be postponed until the next term.

There the matter might have rested but for the fresh memorial sent by Dr Bernard and eighteen other staff members reminding the board of their failure to answer the prayer of the previous memorials. The new petition repeated the same request and added evidence of the experience of 'mixed' education gathered from the hospitals of Dublin and from English and Scottish universities. The evidence highlighted how isolated the Trinity board was in its prejudices. By 1892 every university in Scotland and England, with the exception of Durham, had opened its degrees to women. Oxford and Cambridge had, since 1880 and 1884 respectively, allowed women to attend lectures, sit exams and be placed on the examination lists, although denying them the actual privilege of a degree.

While the board procrastinated, the women's cause was taken up by the academic council of the College. It passed a motion 'that in the opinion of this Council, women should be enabled to obtain degrees in the University of Dublin, provided that arrangements can be made for such degrees and that a committee be appointed to consider and report to this Council how far and in what way such arrangements can be made'.[27]

The board was now faced with a two-pronged attack, one from the CAISM and the other from within the bastion, so to speak, from the junior fellows and professors, both inside and outside of the academic council. It had all the appearance of a tribal quarrel since all the protagonists belonged to that rather small world of Dublin's Protestant academic circle. Ironically the common bond between the adversaries was Alexandra Collge: Alice Oldham and many of the leading CAISM members were teachers there; Provost Salmon and three other members of the board were members of its Council; many of the Trinity staff taught there and numerous Trinity daughters were among its pupils. The common bond notwithstanding, the board fought off the attempt to admit women with a skilful blend of procrastination, hair-splitting and contrived obtuseness.

26. Minutes of the Board, TCD 14 May 1892, xvi, 119 (TCD mun 5/16).
27. Minutes of Council, TCD 1 Mar 1893, i, 398. (TCV v mun 3/1).

1894 passed without any decision being taken, although a deputation consisting of three gentlemen representing the CAISM met a delegation from the academic council and later one from the board. Justice Madden, one of the CAISM representatives, later recounted how all the board was 'opposed to the admission of women to degrees and in fact, scarcely seemed to consider it an arguable question'.[28] Yet the continuous pressure had some effect, and the board sought legal opinion as to their position in the matter. The college solicitor obliged with the view that the statutes 'show that the members of the College and those who pursued their studies should be of the male sex' and suggested that an act of parliament would be needed to effect the change.[28]

The CAISM, while accepting the opinion reluctantly, decided in 1895 to publish the lengthy correspondence which had built up over the two years since the request was first made. The *Irish Times* obliged and a lively correspondence followed in which the board allowed themselves to become involved. They defended their stance with references to their desire to keep in line with Oxford and Cambridge in the matter of giving degrees to women. The fact that both older universities allowed free access to lectures in their men's colleges and to the university examination was ignored. Such an opening was not missed by the CAISM and the board, now hoist with its own petard, was forced into considering how Trintiy could serve women along the lines of the privileges extended by Oxford and Cambridge.

The scheme for admitting women drawn up by a board sub-committee was rejected by the full board who instead accepted the alternative suggested by the vice-provost, J. Barlow. He proposed 'that women should be allowed to be examined in the honour courses for senior freshman year and for the moderatorship examination in the Michaelmas term in 1896 as an attempt to gauge the probable number and ability of women seeking degrees'.[30] The announcement of such a meagre

28. *Royal Commission on Trinity College Dublin and University of Dublin 1906–7*, H.C. 1907 [c.3312] 1.
29. Case for Council on behalf of the Board of Trinity College, to advise with reference to a claim put forward on behalf of females to be admitted as students to Trinity College and to proceed to degrees in the Faculties, conferred by the University of Dublin, (TCD p/1 2489, p. 1).
30. TCD board min., 18 June 1895, xvi, 349–50.

concession was accompanied by a lengthy apologia defending their decision. It read:

> We believe that the teaching of women could not be suitably conducted within the walls of an institution intended for the residence of young men ... since parents who place their sons in residence ... do so in the persuasion that their morals will be subject to some supervision. It has been suggested that female students should be required to be attended by proper chaperons; but it could not be left to the discretion of the gate porters to determine whether of two women passing the gate, one was of sufficient age to be the suitable guardian to the other. If a female had once passed the gate it would be practically impossible to watch what buildings or what chambers she might enter or how long she might remain there. The board have not the least wish to exaggerate the abuses likely to result from the freedom which it is proposed to introduce. They believe the great bulk of our students to be young men of good principles; and the young women whose love of knowledge might induce them to seek education here, would ordinarily be strong enough to resist temptation, but both statements are open to exceptions and cases of scandal might from time to time occur damaging the reputation of the College. Even if no worse evil occurred than parents found the son whom they sent here, early entangled in an imprudent marriage they would not consider that evil small.[31]

The new arrangements met with little approval and support; the lack of teaching created such a daunting obstacle for any student that, without the prospect of the reward of a degree, the exertion would scarcely be justified. The first women to brave the course was a Miss Beatty who in 1900 was awarded a gold medal for her answering on the modern literature papers at the moderatorship examination. Between 1901 and 1903 twenty-three women sat the entrance examination but only one other ventured further.

Colleges for Catholic women
Of the 152 women who had graduated from the Royal University between 1884 and 1892, the majority had received their

31. Copy of Board's statement to CAISM outlining their objections to entry of women, 2 July 1895 (TCD ms 2562 (3)).

education from Protestant schools and colleges, Alexandra, Victoria, High School for Girls in Derry, Methodist College in Belfast and Rochelle in Cork. Only three students listed Catholic schools as their place of study on the degree lists: one came from Dominican Convent, Sion Hill, and the other two from Dominican Convent, Eccles Street; this, however, does not mean that only three Catholic students took degrees. Nevertheless, absence of Catholic schools on the examination lists highlights the Protestant character of the movement.

The lack of enthusiasm in Catholic circles was not unique to Ireland. R. J. Evans in his comparative study of the feminist movements in Europe, America and Australasia establishes that in the case of each movement the impetus for reform came from groups of liberal Protestants in urban circles.[32] The greatest gains were made where Protestantism flourished and correspondingly the least in the Catholic countries. The experience in Ireland bears out his observations. The Catholic middle class was comparatively small in terms of both numbers and influence and its energies were directed towards finding its own political identity. Its educational priorities lay in improving the financing of second-level education and seeking a satisfactory resolution of the university question. These priorities were conceived in terms of the needs of male education only. Female education with the development of the network of religious orders was considered to be in a very satisfactory state.

The Catholic view of the role of women naturally shared many features with the prevailing Protestant conservative views; the notion that marriage and child-bearing fulfil the destiny of a woman; the subordination of a wife to her husband; the rigid division of labour which confined a woman to the domestic sphere and the vilification of the sexuality of womanhood. To these elements the Catholic church contributed a mariology which gave seemingly divine sanction to the subordinate role of women. Mary, virgin and mother, loomed large both in Catholic education and devotional piety. The declaration of the immaculate conception as a tenet of faith in 1854 and the erection of the shrine at Knock in 1879 underpinned these views. The extraordinary expansions of female religious orders reinforced the abstract ideal personified in women enclosed, engarbed and emeshed in a life which

32. Richard J. Evans, *The Feminists, Women's Emancipation Movements in Europe, America and Australasia, 1840–1920* (London 1977), p. 30.

was idealised as the better part, yet who found no role of authority within a male-dominated church. It seems ironic that these women were most responsible for the dissemination of this view of women. Within this context the goals of female education did not rate systematic learning and intellectual development highly. The capture of convent education by the English values of examination and certification is one of the most interesting developments of this period. The fact that Catholic male education had no difficulty at all in this regard merely highlights the difference in the perceptions of the roles of men and women.

The lure of examination fees and the desire to prove that Catholic girls could compete on equal terms with their Protestant peers contributed to the gradual involvement of girls' schools within the Intermediate system. Higher education held fewer attractions and the expense and difficulties of organsing university classes for a small number acted as a deterrent. When challenged, Dr Walsh, Catholic archbishop of Dublin, ruefully admitted that the Catholic answer to women seeking higher education was to send them to a 'Protestant college'.[33] However, the more progressive religious orders gradually began to enter students. Between 1886 and 1892 twelve students from Eccles Street passed second arts, though only two proceeded to take their degree. The greater success of Catholic students who attended Alexandra rankled and the archbishop was called to task by Mother Michael Corcoran, Superior General of the Loreto Order, for his refusal to take action.[34] Against this background it was understandable that when Katherine Murphy, a student of the Dominican convents in Sion Hill and Eccles Street was awarded first place in her MA with the studentship prize of £300, her achievement was celebrated with a *Te Deum* and was hailed publically as a Catholic victory over the Protestants.[35]

In 1893 Dr Walsh sought the co-operation of the Dominican order in the establishment of a Catholic women's college. The Dominicans agreed and later that year St Mary's University College and High School opened with great fanfare. Dr Walsh had planned that the new college would become *the*

33. *Freeman's Journal,* 4 May 1894.
34. Mother Michael Corcoran to Archbishop Walsh, 11 Mar 1893 (Dublin Diocesan archives file 356/4).
35. *Freeman's Journal,* 29 Oct. 1892.

Catholic women's university college.[36] But the Loreto order took umbrage that the Dominicans had been preferred to them. Mother Mary Michael took the initiative herself and designated Loreto College, Stephen's Green, as the university college to serve Loreto schools.[37] In 1894 it opened and soon established its reputation by winning coveted places on the examination results lists. The same year the Ursuline order in Cork opened St Angela's at the request of Dr O'Callaghan, Bishop of Cork.[38]

Though the women's colleges proved their worth yearly by the prominence of their students on the examination lists, their position within the structures of the Royal University were not formalised in any way. No fellow of the University was ever appointed to any of the women's colleges, nor were the colleges represented on the senate. The absence of institutional links cast a shadow over the long-term existence of the colleges. Their survival depended on the continued existence of the Royal University as an examining body. Yet the long-term existence of RUI was itself in doubt. It had always been regarded, by friends and foes alike, as a temporary halting stage in the search for a solution to the vexed university question. Any final solution was expected to include attendance requirements as a prerequisite for the awarding of degrees. At such a stroke the women's colleges, both Catholic and Protestant, would be faced with immediate closure, and Protestant women would be offered the unpalatable choice of a degree in a Catholic university or no degree at all. If developments in England had shaped the foundations of women's university education in Ireland, it was to be the Irish university question which would determine its future.

The demise of the women's colleges

In preparation for tackling the university question the Conservative government appointed the Robertson Commission in 1901 to examine the workings of the Royal University. A similar move was made by the Liberal government which established the Fry Commission in 1907 to examine the affairs of Trinity College. Both commissions presented the CAISM

36. Sion Hill Annals, Nov 1893, p. 196.
37. Mother Michael Corcoran to Archbishop Wash, 17 July 1893 (DDA file 356/4).
38. The records of St Angela's were destroyed by fire in the 1950s.

and the women's colleges with the opportunity to state their views as to the desired future of women's higher education.

In response to a questionnaire sent to its members by the CAISM a new association was set up to represent women's university interests. The Irish Association of Women Graduates and Candidate Graduates (IAWG) was inaugurated at a meeting held in March 1902.[39] Alice Oldham became the first president and Mary Hayden was appointed vice-president.

In the evidence presented to both commissions a deep split emerged between the associations on one hand and the authorities of the women's colleges on the other.[40] St Mary's proved the only partial exception. Under the influence of Mary Hayden it supported the views of the associations at the Robertson Commission but later reverted to the position held in common with the other women's colleges.

Although the women's colleges had been established to meet a need which had been both created and left unfilled by the Royal University, the *ad hoc* nature of their response had, with the passing of time, hardened into a belief in the value of women's colleges *per se.* In the case of Alexandra College the expense of running university classes for small numbers had in 1884 made the council reconsider its involvement in such a venture. Fear of loss of pupils at the senior end of the secondary school plus pride in the achievement of their university students led the council to decide to continue the classes and to allow the costs to be borne by the secondary department. Henrietta White, headmistress of Alexandra College, her views set by her own education in England, cemented these decisions by her often declared belief that only in a women's college could female students experience the full corporate life of a university student. Margaret Byers shared her views and in the case of her college, so much her own personal creation, was reluctant to see the department which had conferred such lustre being terminated in favour of integrated education. Likewise the Catholic church favoured single-sex colleges as providing the best means for the higher education of female students. In the evidence Mary Hayden presented on behalf of St Mary's College at the Robertson Commission she argued for the trans-

39. *Report of the commissioners of university education Ireland, 1901–3,* Document LI (2), iii, 563.
40. For evidence to the Robertson Commission, see *Report of the commissioners on university education in Ireland, 1901–3,* i–iii.

formation of the women's colleges into tutorial-cum-resident-ial halls, a sort of half-way stage between separate and integrated education.

Ironically, it was their own alumnae as well as members of their staffs who decisively rejected the whole idea of women's colleges. All too conscious of the isolation of the colleges, their restricted curriculum, and most of all the danger of their degrees being labelled second class, they strongly argued in favour of women having access to the best university teaching available. Agnes O'Farrelly, representing the Irish Association of Women Graduates (IAWG), bluntly declared on behalf of her members, 'We don't want women to be shut into womens' colleges.' In the uncertain future of university institutions in Ireland the best guarantee for women lay in their full admission to university colleges. These views decisively weakened the case for the women's colleges and in the final report of the Robertson Commission, the commissioners came out in favour of the views expressed by the women's associations.

The admission of second and third arts honours students to some of the fellows' lectures in University College without any catstrophe striking either the male student body or the Jesuit community likewise undermined the position of the women's colleges.[41] It was pressure from the college council which forced Fr Delany into this concession. The new students were drawn largely from St Mary's and Loreto and they combined their classes in their respective colleges with lectures in University College. Their college authorities clearly made no objection, unlike in Belfast where Margaret Byers had consistently opposed her students' attending lectures at Queen's College.

An even greater blow to the whole concept of women's colleges was administered by the admission of women students to Trinity College in 1904.[42] With the passing of time, death had resulted in major changes in the membership of the board of the College. Dr Salmon, though even more obdurate in his old age, could no longer dominate the proceedings of the board. In 1903 Dr Mahaffy successfully introduced a motion in favour of the admission of women. Though Salmon resisted the implementation of the motion with every device in his power it proved to be of no avail. A few days after the King's

41. McKenna, *Delany*, p. 289.
42. TCD Board min., 11 Jan 1902, xvii, 276.

never had to suffer the sight of female students in the precincts of his beloved college.

The alacrity with which students from Alexandra College availed of the new opportunities dealt the death-blow to the college department. Miss White, with the support of Dr Bernard and that section of the Trinity staff which favoured the admission of women to degrees in Trinity but preferred their education be organised separately in Alexandra College, fought the arrangements valiantly.[43] But with the graduation of each succeeding set of women and the building up of social and sports activities for women students and the provision of a lady registrar and hostel her arguments became increasingly irrelevant.

The passing of the Universities Act in 1908 was responsible for the dissolution of the remaining women's colleges.[44] The new act established two universities, Queen's University in Belfast and the National University with three constituent colleges in Dublin, Cork and Galway. (Trinity College remained unaffected.) Under the terms of the act women had total equality with men, not merely in the matter of teaching and degrees but also in staff appointments and university authorities. As was expected an attendance clause obliged all candidates for degrees to attend one of the colleges to qualify for their degree. Provision was made in both universities for affiliated colleges other than those named in the act, which if recognised would be permitted to grant degrees, under the aegis of the university authority.

The autonomy granted to such colleges was considerable. A recognised college could organise its own courses, and set its own examinations monitored only by the adjacent university college. Because of such freedom, stringent regulations were laid down to govern recognition. Birrell, Chief Secretary of Ireland, in outlining the provisions, defended the conditions on the grounds that he was anxious to avoid the new university becoming a 'conglomeration of secondary schools'.[45] Recognition could only be granted to an institution if the college apply-

43. Both outlined their case at great length to the Fry Commission, see *Report of Commission on Trinity College and the University of Dublin,* 1906 [c-3174-6] H.C. lvi, 601 and 607; 1907 [c-3311-2], xli, 1, 87.
44. 8 Edw. 7, ch. 38.
45. Hansard 4, H.C. clxxvi, 349 (31 Mar 1908); Statutes for National University of Ireland, 1909 (160) lxix 189.

ing was not involved in any way in secondary education. It had to have an adequate number of students and a well-qualified teaching staff with all the facilities needed for the proper teaching of the subjects offered. The application had to be made in the first instance to the senate of the NUI who would pass it on, in the case of colleges in Leinster, to the governing body of University College, Dublin, for a report. Their report had to be referred back to the senate for the final decision.[46] The implications for the remaining women's colleges, if recognised, were enormous. For those who sought full university status this could provide an answer. But for those who were conscious of the need women had to have their teaching and learning recognised as equal to that provided in men's colleges, the autonomy granted under the act was to be rejected because it would not only further isolate women's education from the mainstream, but would also lower the status of the degree they would obtain, the supervision of the adjacent university college notwithstanding.

Queen's University refused to consider such an arrangement and Victoria College closed its college department in 1909. St Angela's appeared to have taken the same action. However, the authorities in St Mary's and Loreto colleges decided to make an application for recognition, a decision governed by considerations wider than those pertaining strictly to existing debates on the continuation of women's colleges.

Part of the attraction of retaining the colleges lay in their value to both Dominicans and Loreto in providing university education for their own nuns. Without recognition nuns would have to attend lectures in UCD to obtain a university degree. Given the virtual enclosure which their customs dictated, especially in the case of the Dominicans, this was an unpalatable option. Fr P Finlay, a lecturer in UCD who was opposed to the Universities Act, included in his arguments the deterimental effect the proposals would have on the position of women.[47] He singled out the position of nuns, 'who could not',

46. The National University of Ireland, application for the recognition of the College as a recognised college of the University 1910 (St Mary's), (Dominican Archives, Eccles Street, Dublin); Application by Loreto College, Stephen's Green, for recognition as an affiliated college to University College, Dublin, Jan 1910 (Jesuit Archives).
47. Sacerdos, (Fr. P. Finlay), 'Mr. Birrell's University Bill', in *New Ireland Review*, xix, (June 1908) p. 20.

he claimed, 'under any circumstances assist at College lectures'. Added to that, though there was no strict obligation on secondary teachers to have degrees, the maintenance of the high teaching standards for which both orders were famous made it a matter of some importance that nuns should continue to have access to university education. The qualifications of the teaching staff in Alexandra, now raised by the influex of the first Trinity graduates, added an edge to this argument. There was also the fear that the Teachers' Registration Council, which had been set up in England, would be established in Ireland which would make degrees for teachers not just desirable but also compulsory. All these factors galvinised not only the orders but also the hierarchy, who had never previously concerned themselves much with women's higher education, into action. Their entry into the fray lent considerable pressure to the applications which both colleges submitted in 1910.

The IAWG threw its weight against the applications and canvassed individual members of the senate. Norah Meade, an alumna of St Mary's, organised a counter-campaign. She fired her opening shots in an article in the *New Ireland Review* favouring separate education of men and women.[48] Although she stressed that men and women should be on perfectly equal terms as regards the obtaining of all prizes and distinctions, she nevertheless claimed that women would be best educated in separate colleges. Her argument rested on the assertion that the essential differences in the modes of thought and mental development of men and women demanded separate education. Her article provoked a reply from Mary Hayden and Hannah Sheehy Skeffington who dismissed her arguments with the comment,[49]

> if women will not consent to eat at a common table provided for men and women alike, it will, we fear, be their fate to go hungry or to be obliged to content themselves with a few crumbs and husks flung to them in half contemptuous charity.

Undeterred, Norah Meade set up the Irish Women's Educational Association to represent those who shared her views. The new association castigated the IAWG for its desire to

48. Norah Meade, 'Women in University', in *NIR* i, no. 4 (Jan 1907) p. 236.
49. Mary Hayden and Hanna Sheehy Skeffington, 'Women in University, A Reply', in *NIR* i, no. 5 (Feb. 1908), p. 272.

impose co-education. They went further and organised the signing of a petition which attracted three thousand names, a considerable body of support though drawn from circles wider than those concerned strictly with education.[50]

Not all those petitioned agreed to their plea. In a most caustic vein, the bishop of Sligo wrote to Mother Peter of St Mary's College explaining his refusal;[51] he described the memorial as 'the petition of your sweet girl graduates' and judged that if it was met that it would lead to a 'second staff of lecturers, a second staff of Examiners and the setting up of a different standard of knowledge for men and women' which he found unacceptable. In a final trenchant comment he declared that, 'in no university outside Tennyson's *Princess* as far as I know has such a system as this petition suggests been thought of'.

The governing body of UCD rejected both applications, dissatisfied particularly with the close relationships between both colleges and their attached secondary schools as well as the poor emoluments and lack of tenure among the non-religious teaching staff. The senate agreed to abide by this recommendation.[52]

Advised by the reservations of those who had made the decision which stressed the difficulties of recognising two colleges so similar in every way, the bishops' standing committee recommended that just one application be re-submitted.[53] But here they ran up against the refusal of the orders to merge and establish one women's college.

In the face of such obduracy the hierarchy swung its support behind a fresh application from Loreto College which sought recognition for first year arts courses only. Although Archbishop Walsh had made it very clear that two applications would kill the chance of separate women's education altogether, the Dominicans were incensed at being passed over by the hierarchy in favour of the Loreto order. Contrarary to his most expressed wish they too submitted an application.[54]

50. Memorial to the Senate of NUI and the Governing Body of UCD praying for the recognition of a separate college for women, organised by the Irish Women's Education Association (Dominican archives).
51. Bishop of Sligo to Mother Peter, 4 April 1910 (Dominican Archives).
52. Minutes of the Council of UCD, 19 April 1910.
53. Minutes of the General Meeting of the Irish Catholic Hierarchy, 21 June 1910 (Archives of Bishop of Meath).
54. NUI sen. min., i, 279.

The sustained pressure on the governing body of UCD resulted in a reversal of its earlier decision and recognition of first-year arts courses for a limited period of time was granted.[55] However, the board of studies of the senate maintained its objections and advised the senate to take legal advice. This advised against the acceptance of the applications on the grounds that 'no institution belonging to a body which was anywhere engaged in secondary education could be recognised'.[56] Despite the bishops' attempt to question the validity of such advice the senate chose to abide by its opinion.

Thus ended the last remaining women's colleges. The problem of the nuns was solved by a relaxation of their customs and by the mid-1920s nuns began to attend college lectures on a regular basis. Agnes O'Farrelly, though one of the most vehement opponents of the women's colleges, nevertheless acted as their unofficial guardian and secured a separate social room for their use.[57]

Conclusion

The integration of women into the male university colleges fulfilled the most radical demand made by the Irish movement for women's higher education. Yet integration did not bring the full participation of women within the colleges and universities in its wake. The regulations governing women students in Trinity were so restrictive that one can describe their position in the college as being marginal. Though every position was open to women in the National and Queen's Universities, both institutions have remained male bastions where appointments to staff and governing authorities are concerned. Yet the importance which the association attached to the issue of integration was understandable. The status of women's education was at stake. In a patriarchal society only the integration of women into a men's college could guarantee the rating of women's higher education as equal.

The movement for the higher education of women was essentially middle class. The bourgeois presumptions of the role of women in society were left unchallanged. Indeed, the arguement that a better educated woman made a better mother

55. UCD council min., 1 June 1911.
56. NUI sen. min., ii, 310.
57. Information from Sr M. Evangeline MacDonald, Loreto Convent, Crumlin.

was frequently used in defence of women's demand for access to higher education. Marriage and child-bearing remained the unchallenged goals for women and women graduates who worked automatically gave up on marriage. Even the employment available to women after thirty years of the Royal University remained within the mould. The predominance of language and literature in girls' secondary schools largely predetermined the subject options at university level. A BA naturally, so it seemed, lent itself to teaching, a profession long considered to be respectable for women of the middle classes who had to work. The professions remained the preserve of the males of the class. The numbers of women taking medicine and law were so small that they failed to constitute a challenge to this male dominance. The fact that the majority of women graduates got married and did not enter into the employment market or else were given independent means by their families further prevented women earning the due rewards for their academic excellence. The appointment of Mary Hayden as a senator in NUI and as a member of the governing body of UCD, a position she shared with Agnes O'Farrelly, while laudable as a gesture, did not result in an influx of females to the staff. Certainly to have women employed at university level represented a significant breakthrough. Yet the numbers of women employed have never been in proportion to those who have achieved academic brilliance.

The women involved in the movement between 1873 and 1909 were no radical revolutionaries dedicated to breaking the bourgeois mould of the educational or social structures of their society. The most radical and political among them threw their energies into the suffragette cause along with Hanna Sheehy Skeffington or became absorbed in the multiplicity of national movements generated by the Gaelic League or figured in Inghinidhe na hÉireann.

Yet, the movement for women's higher education can claim significant achievements. The lobby organised by Isabella Tod ensured that females were not omitted from the Intermediate and University Acts of 1878 and 1879. With the foundation of the CAISM and later IAWG women took charge of their own educational concerns. They formulated policies which they represented to government commissions. They acted as watchdogs ensuring that the benefits extended to women by the Royal University Act were not erroded. Their espousal of the principle of integration helped to prevent the relegation of women's higher education to second-rate status. Less tangible, but of great significance, was their work in winning acceptance of the idea of higher education for women. This is particularly true in the case of Catholic women. The success of the Protestant colleges in the Royal University examinations posed a challenge to Catholic education. The sight of Catholic women attending Protestant colleges added edge to the desire to prove that Catholics could equal and better Protestant attempts. However, though Catholic orders took up the challenge with considerable success, Catholic Ireland never fully embraced the goals of higher education. In the long term this helps to explain the failure of the movement to build on the achievements won during this phase of the women's movement.

This was not the sole reason. The conjunction of forces which had made the achievements possible — Irish Protestant liberalism, the English Liberal party and Irish and English feminism, did not survive. As time passed the benefits conferred on women were subject to great pressure and it proved all that women could do to hold on to the advantages already conceded. The outbreak of World War I led to the eclipse of the women's movement as a whole. The national struggle from 1916–1922 resulted in the ascendancy of Irish nationalist ideas with their strong vein of social conservatism nurtured in Catholic rural Ireland. It is to these events that one must look for an explanation of the time-gap between the first and present phases of the women's movement. The activities and ideas of that generation of women were peculiar to their time. With the setting up of the new state other forces came into play and the more traditional, Catholic image of women gradually came to dominate. Yet the victories of that generation provided the springboard for the present movement.

Our Age of Innocence

GRÁINNE O'FLYNN

Innocence as a leading female characteristic and a mode of action is projected as an ideal for Irish womanhood. This projection is made by powerful institutions which are, and have been, positively engaged in its promotion. The most obvious institutions are economic, political and religious, and the focus here is on Roman Catholic education.

The Oxford Concise Dictionary tells us that innocence relates to young children; an innocent is a person who is 'simple, guileless and harmless'. Simple, guileless, harmless people do not extrapolate from what they have learned in order to confer meaning on past experience and envisage parameters for future action. An innocent is a person to whom things happen; a person who is not knowingly and actively involved with the practical shaping of her or his living.

The idea of the inherent good of a state of innocence and its link with a childlike state, is detected comparatively late in the development of social ideas in continental Europe. Philippe Aries in *Centuries of Childhood* suggests that it cannot be detected until the last quarter of the seventeenth century.[1] In Ireland, the positive projection of the idea did not become apparent until much later: institutional reinforcement was not obviously given until the middle of the nineteenth century. Both in Ireland and in Europe the churches played an important part in the projection process, and, in both instances, their involvement was related to economic change. The collaboration between the churches and economic forces might be seen as engagement in bringing disorganised and dissatisfied populations to heel. One of the results of church intervention was stimulation of the notion that innocence was a leading behavioural characteristic — a 'natural' characteristic — of women. If we look briefly at the concerns of the re-organised Catholic church in Ireland after the famine, and at new social and economic arrangements, some concrete examples of intervention might be cited.

1. Philippe Aries, *Centuries of Childhood,* Penguin Books, Harmondsworth, 1973, especially chapters 2, 3, and 5.

Historical background

After the famine of the mid-1840s there was a rapid decrease in domestic industry in Ireland and a change in the type of agricultural work. Women become more economically dependent on men, because the opportunities for independent work collapsed.[2] Around that time the conservative churchman Paul Cullen returned to the country from Rome as apostolic delegate and subsequently became archbishop of Dublin and a cardinal. He set about a rigorous reorganisation of the parishes and dioceses of the Catholic church in Ireland. The church's emphasis on the virtue of female docility from this time onwards must be seen in the context of the new economic order and the need to control population growth, as well as in the context of Victorian morality.[3] Dr Cullen's new administration of parishes and dioceses, a growing number of schools for women organised by nuns and sisters, and the deflated population all gave the new philosophy of docility impetus.

As the theoretically non-denominational first-level schools became denominational in practice, as educational opportunities for women increased with the establishment of the Intermediate Board (which established public examinations for post-primary students) and the Royal University in 1878 and 1879, and as control of the teacher education colleges passed into religious hands, the number of religious women engaged in education expanded rapidly.[4] Many female religious were, within their own organisations, outstanding administrators and teachers. But their orders approved of obedience and 'offering it up' and many nuns must have been frustrated by a lack of access to wider spheres. Acceptance of individual frustration was of paramount importance to the harmonious

2. Joseph J. Lee, 'Women and the Church Since the Famine' in Margaret MacCurtain and Donnach Ó Corráin (eds), *Women in Irish Society,* Arlen House, Dublin, 1978, pp 37–46 (hereafter referred to as *MacCurtain and Ó Corráin*); Margaret MacCurtain, 'Towards an Appraisal of the Religious Image of Women' in *The Crane Bag,* Vol. 4, Dublin, 1980, pp 26–30.
3. *Ibid.*
4. For analysis of the change from non-denominationalism to denominationalism in the national school system, see Donald Akenson, *The Irish Education Experiment,* Routledge and Kegan Paul, London, 1972; John Coolahan, *Irish Education: History and Structure,* The Institute of Public Administration Dublin, 1981. Gráinne O'Flynn, 'The Education of Irish Women' in *The Capuchin Annual,* Dublin, 1976, might also be useful.

administration of each institution. Docility was a commended trait in each nun and it is not surprising that inculcation of a similar trait in female students became a discernible educational objective. The moulding of docility and its practical expression — unquestioning obedience — is an educational aim which requires clear delineation of the boundaries of what is taught and tends to control the desire to question. It attempts to negate individual dynamism and to promote group stasis. Behavioural rules also play an important role in this process. In a culture informed by religious beliefs the process becomes more powerful if educational strategies are presented as being responsive to those beliefs.

As religious women became increasingly involved with the education of females in Ireland, schools began to assume a religious ethos even though displays of religious objects were forbidden in state-endowed schools until the twentieth century. The very presence of nuns as teachers appeared to confirm a relationship between what was taught and a divine plan.

The educational system, by complementing the church's emphasis on female docility, which in turn served economic ends, aided the containment of more than half the Irish population, apparently through its own acquiesence.

It was only when there were divisions within the churches — particularly in the majority Catholic church — on, for instance, the land question and on the future constitutional status of the country, that women emerged in the public arena in an active way.

In the last decades of the nineteenth century and in the first quarter of the twentieth century, during times of church and political disharmony, political statements of intent on a new Ireland made no distinctions between the future place of women and men within it.

Ireland was one of the first countries in the world where women won suffrage; in the years 1910 to 1923 some women began to emerge as prominent public figures. However, after the independence struggle had ended, women disappeared from the public scene.[5] This situation can be compared with the pre- and post-independence status of many women in emerging nations. Official approval is given to women's involvement

5. See Margaret MacCurtain, 'Women, the Vote and Revolution' in *MacCurtain and Ó Corráin,* pp 46–58.

with the nationalist/liberation cause during a period of conflict. When, however, constitutional negotiations begin and the public order changes, there are rapid public attempts to direct our return to states of docility. And as Rosemary Radford Ruether has pointed out, during times of war, all the communications media reverse their usual messages and call on women to become surrogate men as truck-drivers and workers in heavy industry. After the war, however, we are told to make room for returning males, who have a natural prior right to the jobs, to be obedient and to produce babies to replace the slaughtered population.[6]

The process is often ratified by two extra-worldly public stances: that taken by religious leaders and that taken by the new political élite. The religious leaders overlook the involvement of women in the pre-independence struggle or relegate it to the status of a best-forgotten deviation; a return to innocence is the best way to erase it from popular consciousness. The political élite look into their own hearts and set out to construct a mythical 'golden age' where women are comely, non-vocal producers of magnificent men. Their arguments are elevated to extra-terrestrial dimensions by their claims to exclusive knowledge of the 'golden age' and their subsequent public acclaim.[7]

When I started to go to school in Dublin in the 1940s, twenty years after independence, the social moulding process of women as innocents had been firmly re-established.[8] Ireland had a new constitution; new suburbs were being built as were new schools and parishes, but it appeared as if the involvement of women in preparing the way for this new Ireland had never happened. With hindsight, religious and political directives to women were primarily concerned with encouraging our return to mid-nineteenth century status. The following section of this paper is based on individual experiences, but I believe them to be more than a subjective part of a social process, and official pronouncements as outlined in the subsequent section reinforce my claim.

6. Rosemary Radford Ruether, *Sexism and God-Talk,* SCM, London, 1983, especially chapter 4 (hereafter referred to as *Ruether*).
7. For a wide-ranging discussion of the idea of the political elite and the return to a 'golden age' see T. B. Bottomore, *Elites and Society,* Penguin Books, Harmondsworth, 1969.
8. See Article 42.2, 1 and 2, *Bunreacht na h-Eireann,* The Stationery Office, Dublin, n/d, pp 136–8.

My education and upbringing

My parents had married in the late 1930s. They went to live in a
new suburb in Dublin. They had two children. Our family was
small in comparison with the rest of the families in the suburb,
except for Protestant families. Protestant families were not a
large component of the population — about five per cent — but
by the age of six I was aware of differences between us. Originally, awareness came from a myth — fortified to a degree by an
accident of geography — that all Protestants lived only on the
north side of roads. The second and most pervasive aspect of
difference related to school attendance, church attendance and
patterns of social activity.

Catholic church activity impinged greatly on our lives.
Parish priests and curates concerned themselves with families
and schools. Separate women's and men's sodalities were set
up, as were committees to raise funds to pay off church debts.
For many women the sodalities and the committees became
focal social centres. There was an obvious competitiveness
between members. This arose from the production of goods for
church sales and also from interest in entertaining local clergy.
We children could point out houses which were visited by
clergy and where crustless sandwiches and sugar-dusted
Victoria sponge cakes were served to them on wedding-present
china. The visits led to increased standing for the hostesses in
the neighbourhood and also to status for their children in local
schools if they were picked out with kindness by visiting
priests.

Catholic schools were new in the area and they were run by
orders of nuns. Boys came to school with girls until they
reached what was called 'the age of reason', but really the age
of seven. Our first formal encounters with religion were made
at school. More pervasively, our institutional socialisation into
what it meant to be Catholic women began there. At first,
probably because they looked so strange, we looked on nuns as
being apart from the rest of humanity. Although we grew used
to how they looked, we grew more convinced of their remoteness. They did not live in ordinary houses; they had to be
accompanied by other females when they walked in the streets;
they had exotic names; they were 'brides of Christ'. The otherworldliness which enveloped their lives added a mysterious and
forceful dimension to their statements. Occasionally some of
us were cheeky to nuns, but we knew from an early age that to

argue with a nun would be a most grievous transgression.

Young nuns often taught the infant and senior infant classes. We sometimes caught glimpses of favouritism directed by them at beautiful little girls and engaging little boys. Was this a long-suppressed desire for an ideal child which had got momentarily out of control? We hadn't the wit to form the question, but we were affected by the behaviour because the criteria by which we were judged were clear: engaging little boys were articulate little boys; beautiful little girls were clean, curly, docile and silent. From our first days at school we were sexually segregated in our classrooms. Commingling was represented to us as shameful. Often punishment procedures involved a blushing walk across the room to sit among members of the opposite sex. Energetic, exuberant little girls went to the boys' side: boys who wept were sent among the girls. We accepted the procedures without question and carried ideas of suitable female/male behaviour with us beyond the gates of the school.

Protestant friends attended different schools. They were not taught by nuns; their school principal was a man. Girls and boys stayed together in the national school until their final year. Their church involvement percolated more formally into their social lives than ours did. Whereas Protestant clergy did not need to involve the women of the parish in fund-raising activities to the same degree as Catholic clergy — their church was an old one — they did concentrate on youth organisations more than their Catholic counterparts. They had Sunday school, but what we envied most was the Girls' Brigade. The brigade sanctioned exciting physical sports. Members had uniforms; they were arranged in troops; they had secret codes; they had an *ésprit de corps.* It all appeared to be daringly physical and independent. At the brigade's annual display our Protestant friends were awarded badges and medals for gymnastic feats which were prohibited to us by parents and teachers. These centred on rope-climbing, high-jumping and vaulting. And, envy of all envies, shorts were an approved part of their gym uniforms. Some nuns at our school had told us that Our Lady wept when girls wore shorts or trousers.

As we grew older and our social lives moved beyond the confines of our immediate area, the differences between our socialisation as Catholic women and that of our friends as Protestant women became more noticeable. During our middle years at secondary school, my Catholic school friends and I became expert at plotting the routes to and from school which held the maximum possibility for meeting with boys. It was possible on my bicycle journeys to cross roads leading to four boys' schools. The immediate objective was encounter and banter, but the general aspiration was to become a member of a 'mixed' group. Occasionally, some of us were invited by boys to the local cinema on Sunday afternoon. The meetings were arranged and took place without any parental consent.

Our Protestant friends did not become involved in our adolescent adventures. Firstly, there were no Protestant schools for boys on the way to their secondary schools. Secondly, it would have been entirely outside their terms of reference, and ours, if they, even at that age, had shown interest in Catholic boys. Thirdly, and perhaps most importantly, their parents approved of male/female relationships for young people long before ours did. Family outings and church outings were organised by their elders from about the age of fourteen. Although as children we had participated with our Protestant friends in birthday parties and other celebrations, as our interests positively shifted from jelly to men, the Catholic parties ceased and the Protestant ones became denominationally selective.

Without having more than naming knowledge of *Ne Temere* (the Catholic prohibition on mixed marriages unless there is an express promise to bring up the children as Catholics), I accepted this situation albeit reluctantly. The reluctance was many-faceted. I was annoyed at what appeared, even then, to be irrational bias; I was envious of parental approval of 'mixed' parties; I was dying to meet people called Hedley, Clive or Alan. I was convinced that I would be devastatingly witty in conversation with them. Hadn't my entire diet of extra-school reading centred on their prototypes in the *Girls Crystal* and the Abbey and Chalet School books? Hadn't my illicit cinema-going made me conscious of the type of articulate woman who would attract them? They would call me 'old thing'; the friendship would deepen into inseparable companionship; this would (after some minor misunderstandings) blossom into love. From the wealth of experience which I had built up, this appeared infinitely more acceptable then being called 'Stretch' or 'Yeats' (I was five foot nine and into poetry) by Brendans and Séans.

With hindsight, it is possible to isolate some factors which contributed to the tension which grew between the images of our expectations and the reality of our existences. The images were those of innocents. They emanated from our educators, from fiction and from unreal, romantic aspirations of parents and teachers. They had little basis in reality, but reality, which had been avoided in our development process, was what we had to cope with. Before we perceived the dichotomy, some of us imagined that the reality we experienced was a localised distortion and that true life was to be found beyond our Dublin suburb.

By some circuitous reasoning process plus an unarticulated revolt against tradition, a friend and I decided that men in Trinity College held the key to our realisation as companionable women. We were seventeen, still at school, and we concentrated on an immediate possibility — entrance to a dance in the Dixon Hall in Trinity — rather than a long-term improbability — entrance to a degree course.

We planned with some determination to achieve our goal. We had to find out how to get in and how to get out. We had never been inside the gates of Trinity in our lives. We knew no-one who was or who had been a student there. We were aware of memories of British troops in Trinity's College Park in 1916 and of a flying Union Jack in our lifetime. We were also aware of an episcopal ban. We argued ourselves out of the ban. After all, going to a dance was quite different from attending a course of lectures. We did a daylight topographical survey from the college's Front Gate to the Lincoln Place Gate. We quashed the memories. At the dance we met two students who invited us for tea in their rooms on the following morning. The civilised nature of the invitation recompensed for a major disappointment — their names were Michael and Johnny — and a minor one — they couldn't pronounce ours. On the following morning we wore gloves and appeared at 11 am. We were given mugs, which we thought very chic, and a rather uneasy conversation began. It centred on who we were and who they were. When we discovered that they were both sons of clergymen our courage collapsed, the folk memories revived and we left trailing uneasy excuses. Unlike other adventures, this one was never recounted to our friends. We realised that we had gone beyond the bounds of any imaginable limits. There was also the danger that some one might change the name of the beverage to soup.

In spite of the fact that we generally enjoyed our illicit activities, most of us experienced periods of guilt. We were fearful of the shadows of sin which appeared to surround the area of male/female relationships. We didn't talk to our parents because our parents didn't know what we were doing. Their references to sex were usually limited to vague talk about seeds and mysterious implantations. Because of this vague home atmosphere, the school 'retreat' (a period of withdrawal, usually involving religious lectures and conducted by visiting priests) became a focal point for questions about sex. In our school, the two senior classes were given what was called a 'special' session and written anonymous questions to the retreat director were allowed. What we all wanted to know was, was it a sin to kiss?.

The replies had a pattern. First, we were warned about 'the world'. Then we were warned about our sex. The warnings were couched in obscure language and delivered in dramatic tones which thrilled but did not enlighten us. References were made to the arousal of passion, provocative female dress, perfume and 'challenging talk'. Since neither biology nor any science was taught to us, and since our reading was extremely limited, we were quite vague about what arousals meant. We did realise, however, that our normal dress — tightly tied navy gymslips, lisle stockings and gaberdine coats — was highly unlikely to be provocative. Perfume as a stimulus to wild male response seemed interesting, though unviable at a distance, and what was 'challenging talk'? However, at the end of 'special' sessions one thing was very clear to us: we were potentially dangerous. The very female form was a source of evil. The best ways to rid ourselves of its encumbrances were to pray, be modest, adopt low vocal tones and become non-argumentative. To most of us the main difficulty with implementing the advice lay in the low vocal tones and non-argumentative enjoinders. We were developing a desire for some kind of intellectual excitement and an interest in debate. Strangely perhaps, one of our intellectual stimuli came from our religion class. We studied Sheehan's *Apologetics* and Kavanagh's *Social Ethics*. Were we being asked to refrain from argument even in the sphere of faith?

Two of us met what we recognised as a real live communist when we were selling flags for the St Vincent de Paul Society in O'Connell Street. He argued that voluntary aid for the poor was a sop to radical political intervention aimed at eliminating all the divisions between the rich and the poor. We experienced thrills of anticipation during his lengthy discourse. We knew that we could reply with answers from Sheehan and Kavanagh. We knew that communists favoured state interference with the natural order. We knew such interference was morally wrong. We knew how to combat communism by an argument using analogies of trees fulfilling their natural potential. We knew that our final telling phrase would be 'The family was there before the state'. But we remembered the prescriptive enjoinders about low vocal tones and non-argumentativeness and remained silent and went, rather sadly, to rattle our flag boxes under the noses of other people in the cinema queue.

When we left school we tried to kick against constraining mores in an ineffectual way. We began to smoke; we wore stiletto heels; we drank expresso coffee in coffee bars. We got jobs which were terminable on marriage and none of us encountered women in positions of decision making. We found no stimulus to argumentative discourse and we reserved whatever remaining tendencies we had for debate for the confrontations we had with our parents when we stayed out late.

Everyone expected us to get married. We learned the significant pattern. He asked you out with increasing frequency. You met him at Clery's or the Metropole. One Sunday you brought him home. He gave you the watch at Christmas. You knew the next was the ring. Parents watched for the signs with some kind of hope. When the pattern had been established, they were relieved. Often their hopes were conveyed to neighbouring friends and relatives.

When I first went to University College Dublin, I met a male engineering student. He shared digs, a duffle coat and a hat with three others. He had ten shillings a week for pocket money. He knew about Sheehan and Kavanagh. He, like me, had 'done' the odd numbers in English prose and poetry for the Leaving Certificate. We could recite bits of Hayden and Noonan's history off by heart together. We met frequently in the centre of O'Connell Street under the third angel flanking O'Connell's statue. He shouted things like 'Good night MISS and THANKS', along the main road of the suburb when he left me home. He gave me a tin of Libby's fruit cocktail and *Portrait of the Artist as a Young Man* for my birthday. The situation was viewed with some alarm by parents and peers.

Tensions which had developed between us and our parents, particularly between us and our mothers during the years between adolescence and marriage, generally disappeared on marriage. After marriage the old mother/child relationship appeared to be reactivated. There appeared to be a common ground — management of household, husband and children. The role of mentor for our mothers seemed to be revitalised.

There are historical reasons peculiar to Ireland, why our socialisation was shaped in this way. Our parents had lived through the political and social devastation of the 1920s. They had faced a new situation of near devastation during the second world war. As a result, they were deeply concerned with establishing stability in their lives. To a marked degree, the desire for stability was basic to their attempts to mould us in a way so that our futures would contain no elements of risk.

Our fathers had clerical jobs and were in many cases the first generation of their own families to have had these kind of jobs. Each one, consciously or unconsciously, wanted to maintain and increase his standing as a middle-class respectable citizen. The desire encompassed family life as well as work life. A family in which, for instance, a wife worked would have been regarded as one which was economically insecure.

For us, as their children, education was accepted as an important component of respectability. It was a passport to security, but perhaps more importantly, there was a significant class relationship between tolerance of time spent in the education system and social standing. In retrospect, perhaps the most important aspect of education was that the tolerance and sacrifice was sexist. Our parents did make sacrifices to send us to second-level schools. They had to pay fees and defer increases in family income while we were there. But the deferment period for girls in the system, in our suburb, was considerably less than it was for boys. It was accepted, without question, that if boys had a certain amount of talent, particularly in an area relevant to a future profession, and further, if they wanted to continue their education in a university, this would be sanctioned. The simple argument was that they, not the girls, would be the future breadwinners. For most girls who had completed second-level education, the next four or five years were regarded as a period in which they should be occupied in a 'nice' job until they got married.

I think that during this period our mothers were often deeply worried about us. They probably feared that we might deviate from the accepted pattern and they tried to contain us. Our deviation would have been both personally hurtful and possibly socially unacceptable. Occasionally I heard mothers voice frustration but this was about housework or the management of income. I never heard anyone compare a life she might have had if she hadn't married with what she was in fact experiencing.

Perhaps our mothers had day-dreams. Many of them read women's magazines and romances from the local library. We read them too, and sometimes longed for the kind of pure, unwavering love which was achieved by the heroines. Out of love for us, did our mothers harbour hopes that we might experience the kind of relationships recounted in the novels?

Church and state as ratifiying agencies

In the wider social sphere, the surburban microcosm was ratified. The leading agencies which ratified behaviours for us — the government and the churches — did not focus on women as active participants in social life. The 1937 constitution enshrined *all* women in the home. Article 41(2) clearly stated the position: 'In particular the State recognises that by her life within the home woman gives to the State a support without which the common good cannot be achieved.'[9] No distinction was made between married and unmarried women; no reference was made to the role of fathers. The practice of political life mirrored the constitution with accuracy. There were no women in the cabinet. To the majority of Irish people it appeared that the country could only be managed by men in long coats and soft hats who had no sex life.

The church's attitude to women impinged more pervasively and potently on our lives. We had encountered interpretations of the attitude when we had been at school and we had learned that there were behaviours proper to each sex. Official decisions lay behind these interpretations. Policy decisions relating to the education of Catholic girls were made each year by our educators at conferences of religious school principals.

9. *Ibid.*

When the reports of the conferences[10] are examined it can be seen, for instance, that the themes of our school retreats — the danger of 'the world' and the danger of the female form — were discussed yearly and that strategies were laid down in order to stimulate our commitment to a defined lifestyle. For the religious principals, 'the world' contained two pertinent educational bodies — the civil service and the universities. Civil service involvement with the education of girls was defined as existing in two forms. The first was in the hands of the Department of Education; the second was in the hands of the Civil Service Commissioners who attempted to recruit females to their ranks. Frequently, religious principals referred to the civil service and to the universities as adversaries. The Department of Education had official power over curricula. Because of content emphases and omissions, female innocents might be tempted to forsake their only destiny as wives and mothers. The condemnations of the principals were clear, and, at times, sarcastic: 'Our present courses are fairly well adapted to the needs of those whose vocation it is to be theoretical mathematicians, grammarians and literary critics ... but the main function of woman is to be a home maker,'[11] stated one principal.

Her position was positively reinforced by the encyclical of Pope Pius XI, *The Christian Education of Youth*. The main argument of the encyclical in relation to the education of women was that since a 'difference of physical organism in inclination and disposition'[12] existed between women and men, the difference had to be maintained in education. It could only be maintained in schools for separate sexes, where basic role differences were reinforced. 'The function of the women is to found a home and rear children; the function of the man is to work for the support of his wife and family.'[13]

Recruitment to the civil service was linked to recruitment to the universities as having a distorting effect on the education and development of young women. It was agreed at one confer-

10. See *Reports of the Conferences of Convent Secondary Schools in Ireland,* for 1930s, 1940s and 1950s (hereafter referred to as *Conference Reports*). The reports were privately printed and can be found, often unfortunately incomplete, in the libraries of the major religious teaching orders.
11. *Conference Report,* 1949, p 60.
12. *Ibid.,* p. 25.
13. *Ibid.*

91

ence that 'a vicious process of deterioration'[14] had been inititated by them. 'A women's place is in the home ... [there] she is queen, when she unspheres herself she becomes a slave. Our Lady spent her life in none of the brilliant spheres for which many girls sigh ... she did her household duties in the little Nazareth home.'[15] Although religious principals had little or no access to university administrators, they did have access to the Department of Education and they used this to act as an important pressure group for change. They were successful in their campaign for the introduction of lower mathematics papers for girls at Intermediate Certificate ('only twenty per cent of girls are bookish,'[16] ran one argument), in their campaign for the inclusion of domestic science papers in state examinations, and in the accuracy with which their ideas were accepted and passed on to students. Irish religious principals were regarded with envy by their English counterparts. A visiting English principal told a conference in 1949: 'It is wonderful to see the power that you have in education. In fact the Nuns have all the power to guide and control education policy. You have the Department of Education in the hollow of your hands.'[17] It must be remembered that although one of the main reasons why 'the world' was not regarded as a proper sphere of female activity was functionally related to the country's economic circumstances, such an explanation was never given. Every statement about the role of women was couched in theological or philosophical language which obscured the main issue and hinged on the idea that female and male responses to 'the world' were genetically endowed and emanated from a god-given natural order.

At conferences, the idea that the female body was dangerous and a source of temptation, which we had heard at school, was produced time and time again: 'Whether he will it or not a man is tempted by the physical charms of woman. The lines of the female body exercise on him a fascination which can easily become an obsession,'[18] a male lecturer told a conference. Responsibility, therefore, for both male and female chastity rested with women. Girls, often innocently, were 'occasions of

14. *Conference Report*, 1939, p 75. The idea was frequently reiterated.
15. *Ibid*, pp 75–76.
16. *Conference Report*, 1949, p. 21.
17. *Ibid*, p 52.
18. *Conference Report*, 1939, p. 34.

sin'; it was encumbent on educators to point this out to them so that they, in turn, might 'guard against sinful looks.'[19] It was mainly for this reason that girls ought not to engage in physical sports nor to wear revealing garments if they did, occasionally, become engaged in an outdoor game. The wearing of shorts, one lecturer went so far as to say, not only was immodest, but also closely related to failure at tennis. She 'who rarely gets a ball over the net will insist on wearing exiguous shorts.'[20]

Surely much of the confusion we experienced at school was the result of the efforts that were made to mould us into idealised Catholic female forms. The efforts took little cognisance of individual differences and accepted, without question, that only one natural female inclination existed and that its fulfilment alone might be validated. Ironies abounded in the situation. Possibly one of the most important was the official fear that the strength of the inclination might vary or be lessened by contact with agents concerned with stimulation of 'unnatural' intellecual or social inclinations. There was also irony in the fact that neither parents, teachers nor clerical administrators acted in any coherent, public *positive* way towards achievement of their objectives. They acted *negatively,* for they condemned female/male relationships and this condemnation coloured our entire adolescence. We were supposed to realise ourselves finally in such a relationship, but not to experience it during formative years. Was there a fear that we might delay, reject or never be selected for marriage if we were given options? Was there a fear that if we had experience of male company, say in a classroom, that we might, subsequently, be more rational and less docile than we ought?

There is special irony in the facts revealed by the statistics of the Department of Education. It can be seen that the success rates for girls at state examinations are higher than for boys, *in spite* of the moulding process. But there is surely tragedy in the fact that so little female potential is being realised.

The tragedy lies in individual experiences as well as in social deprivation. That particular traits, characteristics and behaviours are predicated for each sex stifles a society's dynamism and distorts social response for *both* males and females. However, since the possibility for diversity of social response exists for males, the tension between individuality

19. *Ibid.,* p. 35.
20. *Ibid.,* p. 33.

and social reinforcement is lessened, and so, in theory at least, is the extent of the distortion. For females, where the possibility of diversity does not exist, the main social agencies engage in compensatory programmes.

The Irish State, through our constitution, acts in this way. The churches also act like this, and, since this activity has not been as fully explored as the state's it might be useful to indicate some areas where its effectiveness has been experienced.

Women and the church

A primary directive of churches to women has been for us to reject engagement with the world. Feminist theologians argue that this directive is theologically invalid. Elisabeth Schüssler Fiorenza in *In Memory of Her*[21] points out that in early Christian communities women were leading ministers and disciples. Although the communities' cultural life-settings were in male-dominated hierarchies, the members lived in accordance with an egalitarian principle which rejected distinction between sexes and different ethnic, cultural and religious groups. The communities' ethos was in practical harmony with the liberation message of Jesus. The post-Pauline church, however, drew out restriction rather than liberation from the Christian movement.

Paul, while theologically accepting the egalitarian Christian vision, had modified it, possibly to placate the existing Greco-Roman culture. After his death, his interpretations and adaptations were used to establish patriachal values and sexual dualities in the Christian church. From then on, the authoritative canon of Christian writings and church organisation were those in which women were portrayed as subject to men and excluded from the centre of social and religious life. The practice of marginalising women, Fiorenza points out, cannot claim Jesus as a source.

Outside canonised doctrine and organisation, attempts were made by some Christians to continue the practices of the first communities. The agnostic gospels — those rejected by dominant Christianity — gave women apostolic authority, and the Montanist sect in the second century gave women equal prophetic authority and participation in ministry with men. After the reformation, some left-wing Puritans, the Baptists

21. Elisabeth Schüssler Fiorenza, *In Memory of Her,* SCM, London, 1983.

and the Quakers practised an egalitarian theology but the implications were only for church organisation and not for society at large.[22]

Dominant Christianity, however, engages in a movement to silence women and to remove women from 'the world'. Basically this can be related to a fear of women which owes its roots to Greek philosophy and to the incorporation of that philosophy into androcentric (man-centred) Christian churches. Greek philosophy presented symbols of women as analogous to the 'baser' realms of the human body and men as analogous to the 'higher' realms. The 'baser' realms were the sexual inclinations; the 'higher' realms the intellectual inclinations. For them the intellectual had to struggle to control the sexual. Females tempted the 'baser' realms and therefore presented dangers of debased humanity. In Christianity the concept of the fall names a woman as the temptress and makes women the primary cause of evil. The concept, it can be suggested, has been used to punish women through centuries of subordination. Augustine stated that women were not made in the image of God; Aquinas called women 'misbegotten males'; Luther described women as a subordinate part of the divinely created order. In many instances the only salvation presented by the Christian churches for males was celibacy. Women in male clerical misogyny have often been presented as sin. Directives to women to reject 'the world' can be seen as complementary to desires for male safety.[23]

Quite clearly if males had been celibate and women had lived in marginalised communities, there would be very little Christian history. Historically, images of Mary and the development of mariology can be set against images of women as evil. Traditional mariology presents Mary as a spiritualised human in whose service the burden of being female can be rejected. Traditional mariology comes close to reversing the Eve image of woman as carnal. In Ireland it is traditional mariology which moulded our religious education as women, and, in a social form, characterised an ideal female nature. In essence it states that we are still inherently dangerous, but, if we mirror the presented image of Mary, this may lead both to our own salvation and to that of Irish men. This means that we ought to

22. For detailed analysis of the selection process see *Reuther*.
23. *Ibid*, especially chapter 4.

acquiesce in a culture of silence and accept unquestioningly our preclusion from making diverse human choices.

As women today we may either have rejected traditional theology or have succumbed to it. We may not have explored the possibility of a liberating feminist theology. The reasons for this are manifold. One of the most important is that we are women and both the dominant Christian religions and the cultural ethos are arranged so that we have little or no access to philosophical and theological debate and decision making. Secondly, although most of us have experienced an innocent's moulding process, many of us may have moved from positions of naivety to positions of shrewdness. The move may have been accompanied by socialisation into middle-class attitudes of caution. Exploring a liberating feminist theology and a commitment to it may be hindered by fear. We may be frightened by a possibility of personal disruption; our basic fears may be of change in the comfortable middle-class *status quo*.[24]

The extent of our fears has been illustrated in the last ten years. One of the instances relates to the publication of the document of the Sacred Congregation for the Doctrine of the Faith — *The Declaration on the Question of the Admission of Women to the Ministerial Priesthood*.[25] The immediate message of the document was that women could not be admitted to the priesthood. The arguments used were based on the assumption that a women's physique was defective since it did not mirror that of the male Christ's. A woman, therefore, the document argued, must be excluded from the 'supreme expression'[26] of the apostolic function of the Christian priesthood in the celebration of the Eucharist. The document's final paragraph was an exhortation to women not to become involved with agitation for wordly religious office. We are told to aspire to a spiritual, other-worldly status: sainthood. A palliative sen-

24. For an extensive discussion on middle-class attitudes in the Catholic Church, see Terence Eagleton, *The New Left Church,* Sheed and Ward, London, 1966, especially pp 85–120. Raymond Williams, *The Long Revolution,* Pelican, 1966, is very useful for analysis of attitudes to changes in the *status quo.*
25. The Sacred Congregation for the Doctrine of the Faith, *Declaration of the Question of the Admission of Women to the Ministerial Priesthood,* Vatican City, 1976.
26. *Ibid.*

tence reads: 'The greatest in the kingdom of heaven are not the ministers but the saints.'[27] Women are urged to forget the world, to revert to a 'natural' role of withdrawal and to await reward in the world to come. The Sacred Congregation reinforces attitudes of the traditional theology and reverts to a world/heaven dualism.

Was it fear which lay behind our failure to analyse and discuss the document publicly? Were we frightened of confronting the institution which had played such an important part in moulding us? Were there not factual errors in the document which might be commented on? Did the writers put forward the idea that Jesus was an ordained priest of the Catholic church who began the Christian ordained priesthood and gave power over the Eucharist to priests through the apostles? If they did, might they have been questioned? Was Jesus, for instance, not a rabbi — a lay teacher among the Jews? Did not the Christian ordained priesthood begin many years after this death?

We said nothing. Was our silence one of the greatest tributes which might be paid to our educators? Was it another proof of the effectiveness of their enjoinders to non-argumentativeness?

Our lack of response to the Sacred Congregation was not an isolated incident. When the *Commission on the Status of Women*[28] presented its preliminary report to the Irish government in 1972, the churches as institutions involved with the socialisation of women were not mentioned. As far as I am aware, one commentator only, the mariologist Donal Flanagan, referred to this obvious omission.[29]

Although it is several years since Pope John Paul II paid a visit to Ireland no debate has yet begun on what appears to be a dichotomy between his descriptions of fulfilled human beings and his subsequent separation by sex of methods of human fulfilment. He clearly described both the ideal environment for realisation and realised human beings. The environment created conditions for dignified growth. Human beings would therein be realised as historical, dynamic, social communicators. He made no separation by sex of young people who were

27. *Ibid.*
28. See *Report of the Commission on the Status of Women,* The Stationery Office, Dublin, 1972.
29. Donal Flanagan, 'The More Subtle Discrimination', *Studies,* Autumn, 1975, Vol. LXIV, pp 234–44.

called on to resist indifference to 'temporal, historical injust-ice',[30] nor of those called on to give themselves to the 'service of life.'[31] There was no segregation by sex of those who were enjoined to 'appreciate to the full the dignity and vocation'[32] of being human. He did not talk to males alone. Why then, did he state: 'Irish mothers, young women and girls, do not listen to those who tell you that working at a secular job, succeeding at a secular profession, is more important than giving life and caring for this life as a mother.'[33] Why was work as a mother invested with a spiritual dimension while life in other realms was seemingly *abandoned* as life in the world? Why, for ins-tance, were men and women not asked to accept parenthood as a vocation? Was it because he is a man? Was it because *parental* vocationalism involves two people who might be actively and knowingly concerned with what they are doing and thus making *rational* decisions? Most importantly, why have we not asked him? Are we too naive or too shrewd? Do we hide behind a public guise of innocence if the risk becomes too great?

Conclusions
In the end we can only negate our innocence by showing that it is anathema to us. We need support from each other in order to make a positive impact on religious and social institutions. Rosemary Radford Ruether in *Sexism and God-Talk*[34] suggests that support might be developed by the establishment of auto-nomous feminist groups which are vitalised by the idea of liberation from sexism in religious organisation and social life. From the groups, transformed vision might be brought to bear on the centres of power. This demands commitment and risk. It also appears that in terms of our education process a study of theology and a study of the sociology of religion might be incorporated into second level schools' curricula on precisely the same basis as any other validated subject content area. Particular emphasis might be placed on the facts that biblical texts are historical formulations which have emanated from religious communities, and that what is canonised has been selected and authenticated by human beings. A basic fact

30. See Papal Address, Galway, *The Irish Times,* 1 October, 1979.
31. *Ibid.*
32. *Ibid.*
33. See Papal Address Limerick, *The Irish Times,* 2 October, 1979.
34. *Reuther,* especially chapter 8 and 9.

emerging from such emphasis is that churches are not abstract entities; they are institutions involved in history. In other words, churches, and the teaching of churches, are not inspired institutions which are given. The selection of criteria for organisational principles and correct emphases has been dominated by males. The possibility of developing an alternative interpretative model or a hermenuetics exists when it becomes possible to show that Christian religious organisation and classical theology are based on male tradition rather than on universal human experience. The possibility of seeing that women have been written out of classical theology, particularly in New Testament writings, and that male hermenuetics defined them as subject to men, calls for a new feminist interpretative model. The use of women's experience of religion as a source of religious content and a criterion of truth, it can be argued, are as valid as the use of the patriarchal life settings from which the post-Pauline Christian church developed its experimental models and authoritative role.[35]

Finally, it can be pointed out that projection of the idea that innocence as a leading female trait, as a divine demand of women, is oppressive to women and oppressive to men. It appears that as women, we have to be primary movers in proclaiming the sin of sexism. This may mean that we have to move beyond a safety which we have accepted. We may have to face criticisms and accusations of uncharacteristic behaviour. But it is only by being uncharacteristic that we can begin to shatter the moulding process. Unless the mould is broken we cannot begin to convince ourselves and the power institutions that innocence as a women's leading characteristic is a distortion and a lie.

35. *Ibid*, especially chapter 1.

Schools and Gender Roles

DAMIAN HANNAN AND RICHARD BREEN

Introduction

A 'structural shift', as it has been called, appears to be occuring in economic and social life in Ireland, as in many other western societies. What had become a 'normal' expectation of improving living standards and changing lifestyles can no longer be taken for granted, and what had become a commonsense view of our particular division of labour and authority relationships in work and family life is no longer so commonsensical. Nowhere are these changes more obvious than in adult gender roles, with rapid change in family and work-role patterns for younger married couples, very fast decline in fertility levels within marriage and in the age of completion of childbearing and childrearing, and a decreasing stability in marriage and the course of parental life. So what had been a gradual cumulative process of change in economic and social life from the early 1960s appears now to have become much less secure: the steady expansion of middle-range white-collar employment (particularly clerical employment) has come to an end; the almost universal retirement pattern of younger married women from the employed labour force has become blurred with many more women staying on in employment after marriage, with perhaps a brief break for childrearing, and the previously firm distinctions within the labour market between those jobs open to early and usually vocationally educated school leavers, and those available to later, usually secondary educated (Leaving Cert) school leavers are no longer being sustained. With declining employment opportunities, competition for jobs at all levels is now far more intense: nobody can feel as secure in their conventional niches as previously.

Over the past twenty-five years schools have assumed a central role in economic placement. Even in 1961 only about one in seven of each young cohort went on to do the Leaving Certificate, but by the mid-1980s around two out of three children growing up in Ireland continue to the Leaving Certificate. This shift in education has coincided with shifts in the labour

100

market. Up to the early 1960s a third of our young people inherited family-owned businesses and many others got jobs informally through local or family networks. Today educational performance and credentials are much more important and we have a more formally competitive job opportunity system.[1] As a consequence of such trends rather than as an objective they set themselves, schools have come to play the central sorting and labelling role, as 'credential-giving' institutions, in labour market placement.

The adaptation of educational institutions to these structural changes has been remarkable — particularly in the ten-year period after 1967 when (with the introduction of free second-level education) the number of pupils and teachers in second-level schools almost doubled, and when more and more pupils were staying on at school after the period of compulsory schooling, in senior-cycle courses.

A buoyant labour market in the rapidly expanding industrial and services sector and an equally buoyant marriage boom which, up to the late 1970s, 'created' many job openings, through married women's withdrawal from paid employment into household employment, helped the apparently effortless adaptiveness of schooling. As a result the implicit adult role models for which second-level pupils were being prepared were still comfortably 'traditional' or conventional up to 1980 or so — requiring no great change in the more successful academic, career-oriented goals which had characterised Irish secondary schools since the late nineteenth century.[2] Indeed, accompanying the disproportionate secondary (rather than vocational or technical) school expansion which occurred after 1967, white-collar or non-manual (clerical) employment also increased disproportionately. In other words, labour market and adult role 'demand' and educational 'supply' remained roughly in equilibrium up to the recession of the 1980s.

But since the 1980s began, the growing momentum of the

1. See D. B. Rottman, D. F. Hannan, N. Hardiman and M. M. Wiley (1982). *The Distribution of Income in Ireland: a study in social class and family cycle equalities,* Dublin: ESRI paper no. 9, chapter 2; D. B. Rottman and P. O'Connell (1982) 'The changing social structure in Ireland' in F. Litton (ed.) *Unequal Achievement,* Dublin: IPA 63–88.
2. See J. Coolahan (1981) *Irish Education: history and structure,* Dublin: IPA; V. Greaney and P. Kellaghan (1984) *Equality of Opportunity in Irish Schools: a longitudinal study of 500 students,* Dublin: Educational Company.

recession and the rapid decline in labour demand in areas such as clerical and public service employment, teaching and nursing, have created and will continue to create a serious imbalance in educational 'outputs' and economic and societal 'demands', particularly for female education. There are marked differences in the kind of education received by boys and girls and, by and large, girls' education has been designed to fit them for the traditional areas of female employment (especially clerical work) and the traditional female adult roles of mother and wife. It is in precisely these areas that the greatest changes have occurred. The period of rapid expansion in clerical and related employment was coming to a natural end in any case even if there had been no recession. And very significant changes in the marriage/work-roles of young married couples have radically changed the agenda for schools.

Schools, like other complex organisations, although originally fashioned to fulfil some clearcut objectives, nevertheless gradually 'conventionalise' these objectives into tasks and roles to the point where the adaptive compromises amongst teaching staff, and between staff, management, pupils and parents, become so taken for granted and so shaped to the various interests involved in the running of the school, that the original purposes or goals become no longer a conscious preoccupation of most people involved. What was once original and new has become routinised. Only the shock of its habitual 'products' no longer meeting demand will force a rethinking in many such schools. It is uncomfortable to have to redefine and adapt to new realities, but school roles will have to be rethought and refashioned in the radically different economic and social conditions of modern times.[3]

For such a redesign or reorientation to be effective, however, requires an understanding of the underlying factors that brought about the different types of education now being received by girls and boys, and of what factors, if changed, would bring about the desired changes. In our study[4] we

3. See R. Breen (1984) *Education and the Labour Market: work and unemployment among recent cohorts of Irish school leavers,* Dublin: ESRI paper no. 119.
4. D. F. Hannan, R. Breen, B. Murray, N. Hardiman, D. Watson and K. O'Higgans (1983) *Schooling and Sex Roles: sex differences in subject provision and student choice in Irish post-primary schools,* Dublin: ESRI paper no. 113.

thought it necessary, therefore, first to investigate who made the decisions about sex-differential education — whether it was school decision makers, teachers, pupils or parents; and secondly the bases on which such decisions were made. There would be no point in policies which, for example, attempted to change school provision of subjects if the pupils themselves made the choices rather than the school. Unless we know *where* responsibility for differential education lies, as well as the bases on which such 'decisions' are made — to offer or not offer a subject to a pupil, or, for pupils, to take or not take a subject offered — we cannot effectively intervene to bring about change.

As a result, our analyses have been concerned both to identify the degree and type of sex differences in post-primary education, and to determine where policies might most usefully be directed.

Sex difference in education

One of the most obvious ways in which girls' education differs from that of boys is the fact that they are in different types of schools. Girls are more likely to be in secondary rather than vocational schools. In 1980–1, for instance, 79 per cent of girls in post-primary education were in secondary schools and only 13 per cent were in vocational schools, whereas among boys, vocational schools accounted for 28 per cent of pupils, with a further 62 per cent in secondary schools.[5] In addition, girls are far more likely to stay on in school to the senior cycle. It has been estimated that in 1981 two-thirds of the female cohort, but only half of the male cohort, entering post-primary education went on to do the Leaving Certificate.[6] To some extent the different distribution of the sexes across the school types and the greater propensity of girls to complete senior cycle may arise for much the same reasons. Vocational education and the tendency to leave school after the Group or Inter Certificate (at about fifteen) have traditionally been linked to entry into manual forms of work — both skilled craft work and unskilled labouring work — which are more widely available to males than females. There are other reasons, however, which are less closely tied to the labour market but linked to the broader ex-

5. Department of Education Statistical Report 1980–1, p. 42.
6. Hannan *et al.*, p. 54.

pectations for adult roles for girls. In many instances education for girls is viewed as having rather more to do with the acquisition of orientations and acomplishments in a broad sense — a general Christian/liberal education — than with specific vocational preparation for a lifetime in the labour market.

Perhaps the clearest index of the way in which girls' post-primary education differs from boys' (and thus also the extent to which each has a specifically vocational content) is to be found in the differences in subject take-up between the sexes. The proportions of boys and girls sitting for certain of the Inter and Leaving Cert examinations reveal that there are major differences in the subjects that girls and boys study. In 1980 (see Table 1) there were 24,500 male candidates at Inter Cert, compared with 26,500 female candidates and at Leaving Cert there were just short of 16,000 male candidates and 20,600 female candidates. On this basis alone, then, if the two sexes were distributed evenly across the examination subjects we should expect that, for any subject, a slightly higher percentage of candidates would be female. In fact the true picture, as revealed in Table 1, is very different.

An Inter Cert both higher level maths and science are dominated by boys, commerce is dominated by girls, but far and away the greatest sex differences in take-up are in the applied subjects. Home economics is taken by almost no boys; and mechanical drawing, woodwork and metalwork are taken by virtually no girls. Turning to the Leaving Cert subjects sex differences are generally greater than at Inter Cert — it is almost as if sex roles become increasingly polarised as pupils progress beyond the Inter Cert. For example, in higher-level maths the sex difference at Leaving Cert is much greater than at Inter Cert. The take-up of five Leaving Cert science subjects is given in Table 1: these are physics, chemistry, biology, applied maths and higher-level maths (which we count as 'science'). Of these, biology is the most popular among both boys and girls, 40 per cent of boys and 62 per cent of girls taking it at the Leaving Cert. It is the only science subject that shows greater take-up by girls than boys and indeed is the only senior cycle science that shows much female take-up at all. All the rest are taken by 10 per cent of girls or less. Applied maths is the science subject showing the smallest rates of take-up by either sex — 4 per cent of boys, almost no girls — and it shows the greatest sex difference in take-up. But physics, chemistry and higher-level

104

maths also show pronounced bias towards boys in their take-up.

Of the next three subjects, accounting, business organisation and economics, only economics shows a substantial sex bias, and that is towards boys. This is the most popular senior cycle commerce subject among boys but the least popular among girls. Accountancy and business organisation really show no overall sex bias in their take-up when we take into account the greater number of female than male Leaving Cert candidates.

The greatest sex differences, however, again occur in the take-up of the practical subjects. Technical drawing, like engineering workshop and building construction, is taken by almost no girls. Home economics (general) is taken by almost no boys (though the male take-up rate for the social and scientific home economics course is somewhat higher).

In summary, then, we can point to a number of subjects which show a very clear sex difference in their take-up. Such sex differences tend to be greater at the Leaving than at the Intermediate Certificate. The sciences and the technical subjects are taken disproportionately by boys while subjects like home economics, art, music, and to some extent the modern languages, are taken disproportionately by girls. However, though several subjects show very large sex difference in take-up, the majority are taken disproportionately by boys. In other words, it is in the male-dominated subjects — notably the science and technical subjects — rather than the female dominated subjects that the major sex differences lie.

In attempting to explain such sex differences in take-up we have developed a model which attributes them to the combination of three factors which we term *provision, allocation* and *choice.* And we have attempted[7] to determine what role each plays in accounting for the observed sex differences in subject take-up. By *provision* we refer to the subjects taught in the school. Schools containing girls tend to have different curricula to schools containing boys: our interest is in determining how much of the sex difference in subject take-up is due to this. Even given identical curricula, however, schools may vary in how subjects are *allocated* to pupils. For example, even if a school teaches a particular subject, all pupils may not have equal access to it. In deciding who may take a particular

7. *Ibid,* chapter 5.

subject, or indeed who must take it, schools often draw distinctions between pupils on the basis of sex, or previous performance. Here, of course, our primary focus is on the existence of allocation rules that are explicitly based on sex distinctions within schools, which, for example, may assign technical drawing to boys and home economics to girls. But as well as this, we are concerned with how allocation practices might vary between boys' and girls' schools. For example, are boys' schools more likely than girls' to make a subject such as science compulsory for all pupils? Again, our interest in such differences in allocation practices is related to the question of how much of the sex difference in subject take-up might be due to differences in this area.

Thirdly, we looked at the pupils' own *choices*. Whether a school teaches a subject or not and how a school which teaches a subject allocates it to its pupils, are outside the control of individual pupils. However, when subjects are presented as options to pupils, then the pupil's own choice determines whether or not he or she will take it. Thus, differential student choices could also be important determinants of sex differences in subject take-up. How much of these differences in take-up is due to choice and what underlies such sex differences in choice is one of the main aims of our research.

Provision differences
Our interest in the provision of subjects, then, concentrates on two issues. To what extent do schools containing boys teach a different curriculum from schools containing girls, and what accounts for such differences? If we begin with the junior cycle (up to the Inter Cert level) then what is perhaps most striking here is the relative similarity of schools' curricula. Given that there are fewer Inter than Leaving Cert subjects, and that, by and large, a core group of four or five subjects is taught in all schools to Inter Cert, the scope of curricular variation between schools is correspondingly less. Nevertheless, there are some distinctive differences. Vocational and community or comprehensive schools (which are generally coeducational), for example, have the highest levels of provision in technical subjects. On the other hand, technical subjects are almost entirely absent from girls' single-sex schools. Conversely, in girls' and co-educational schools there is a very high level of provision of home economics, whereas it is almost entirely absent in

106

boys' schools. Finally, although French is taught in almost all schools, a second or even third language is likely only in girls' secondary schools and in some community schools.

At senior cycle (to Leaving Cert level) the curricular differences between schools widen, as one might expect: so the highest levels of science subject provision are found in boys' secondary and community/comprehensive schools. Although almost all vocational schools teach biology, they tend to have the lowest overall level of science provision, primarily because they are small. As at Inter Cert the technical subjects are more strongly represented in the vocational and community/comprehensive schools and are absent from girls' secondary schools. Furthermore, provision levels in this area are rather higher in coeducational secondary schools than in boys' secondary schools. And such schools usually teach one or both of the home economics subjects. If we concentrate then on boys' and girls' secondary schools, we find that at senior cycle boys' schools are in general strong in science and commerce but relatively weak in home economics, art and music and in languages other than French. Girls' schools, on the other hand, tend to be less strong in science and commerce, but have better provision of home economics, art, music and second or third langauges. Neither boys' nor girls' schools are strong in the area of technical subjects, though some boys' schools teach technical drawing and a few teach building construction.

In examining changes in the curricula of boys' and girls' secondary schools over the period between 1968 and 1978 we discovered that although girls' schools have grown more rapidly than boys' they have both added subjects at an approximately equal rate: in other words the greater growth in pupil numbers in girls' schools has not led to a greater expansion of the curriculum. What expansion of the curriculum there has been, however, shows marked sex differences. Boys' schools have tended to expand into the sciences and, to a lesser extent, commerce subjects, whereas girls' schools have been more likely to add languages and subjects such as art, home economics and music.

But aside from the individual subject differences there is another important respect in which boys' and girls' school curricula differ — in the extent of concentration or specialisation. Boys' schools tend to specialise — that is they concentrate their senior cycle curricula into one or two areas such as science and the commerce subjects, whereas girls' schools are far more likely to spread the subjects they teach across the various subject areas, teaching some science, some commerce, some languages, and so forth. This means that in boys' schools the tendency is towards encouraging pupil specialisation in one or two areas, whereas this is less true of girls' schools. It is particularly striking in the case of small schools (of around 300 pupils or less). Whereas a girls' school of this size will have something like two sciences, one or two commerce subjects and one or two languages, art and home economics, the boys' school of comparable size will tend to concentrate on teaching three or four sciences, or two or three commerce subjects. The result is that in boys' school the curriculum is narrow but deep and pupils are almost obliged to specialise, whereas in the girls' school the curriculum is broad and shallow and such specialisation in small girls' schools is almost impossible.

What accounts for these curricular differences? Our own data suggest very strongly that, particularly among secondary schools, decisions of individual school managements have been vital in shaping the curriculum. But of course different policies are associated with different types or organistations of schools. So, for example, vocational schools and community/comprehensive schools each have, as a group, distinctive curricula corresponding to their collective 'charters'. The differences between these schools and the secondary schools are greater than are the differences among vocational schools or among community schools themselves. Within the secondary sector, however, there are very wide curricular variations, and factors like school size, the number of teachers, the location of the school and so on, only account for part of this. Our conclusion is that the school management's own decisions (whether taken by the individual school manager or more centrally by, for example, the religious order that runs a number of schools) about what subjects to add or drop, have been crucial in explaining curricular variation. The background 'curricular agenda' of schools appear to be highly structured and to be very important in subject provision and take-up differences.

Allocation differences
One very obvious source of sex differences lies in the use of sex

as a basis on which to allocate subjects and this is very commonly adopted in coeducational schools. In a representative sample of ninety-five post-primary schools it was discovered that almost four-fifths of vocational schools and two-thirds of community/comprehensive schools and just under half of secondary coeducational schools use sex as a basis on which to allocate subjects to pupils. The usual distinction is along the lines of technical subjects to boys, home economics, art or commerce to girls.

A more concrete example can be found in the Department of Education's Statistical Report concerning the position in vocational schools. For example, there are approximately 205 coeducational or boys' vocational schools in which home economics is taught at Inter Cert, and yet it is offered to boys in only forty-six schools. Similarly, mechanical drawing is taught in approximately 206 coeducational or girls' vocational schools, but is only offered to girls in thirty-one of them.

As well as sex differences in allocation arising in this way they can also come about if boys' and girls' schools adopt different rules about how a subject is to be allocated. Inter Cert science provides a good example of this, as can be seen in Table 2. Again, using our sample ninety-five schools, we can see that virtually all schools teach or provide Inter Cert science, but it is allocated in very different ways in boys' and girls' schools: whereas twenty-one out of twenty-four boys' schools make science obligatory for all pupils, only two out of twenty-two girls' schools do this. In the majority of girls' schools, science is an option either for all pupils or for the higher ability pupils alone. If we go further than this and examine the science options in those twelve girls' schools which offered science as an option to all pupils, then we discover that in six cases it was a straight choice between science and home economics and in the remaining six schools it involved a choice between science and subjects such as commerce, art and music. In other words, not only are boys generally obliged to take science to Inter Cert but girls, if they wish to take science, are being asked to choose it in preference to subjects that are traditionally popular among girls.

Such variations in allociation (at Inter Cert) have some obvious consequences at senior cycle. For example, it is often the case that, for a pupil to be given the option of taking a particular Leaving Cert subject, a school requires that he or she has obtained a specific grade in its Inter Cert counterpart. For example, most schools require a certain grade at Inter Cert science before they will let a pupil take Leaving Cert chemistry or physics. If girls are less likely even to sit for Inter Cert science then it follows that they have less chance of meeting these academic criteria for the senior cycle science subjects. But perhaps the clearest illustration of this is found in the case of technical subjects. Approximately 20 per cent of girls in the senior cycle are in schools which teach technical drawing, but of this 20 per cent only the most minuscule fraction are in a position actually to take it up, since in general to take technical drawing at Leaving Cert pupils are required to have done mechanical drawing to Inter Cert. Bur virtually no girls do mechanical drawing, either because they are not allowed to, or because they would have to choose it in preference to subjects like home economics or commerce.

One final point regarding allocation practices is that boys are, at both junior cycle and senior cycle, given less freedom to choose their subjects than are girls. We have already seen this in the case of Inter Cert science, but it is true of other subjects. For example, in Inter Cert commerce a roughly equivalent number of boys are allocated the subject as obligatory as are offered it as an option, and in mechanical drawing for every four boys given the option of the subject three are obliged to take it. On the other hand, among girls, for every girl who is obliged to take commerce, five are given the option and similarly for every girl obliged to take home economics, five are given the option.

Differences in subject choice

Even allowing for the sex differences in subject provision and allocation it is clear that boys and girls also make different choices of subjects and this can be seen in Table 3. In Table 3 we have taken those boys and girls in a national sample of 4000 Leaving Cert pupils who are qualified to take and who are given the choice of the seven subjects listed and we have examined what percentage of them avail of this opportunity. So, for example, of these boys who may do physics if they wish, 53 per cent actually do so as against 17 per cent of girls; that is a boy/girl ratio for this 'true rate of choice' as we call it of roughly 3:1. In other words, boys are three times more likely than girls to take up physics when given the choice. Similarly,

110

boys are more likely to choose chemistry, higher maths and technical drawing, whereas girls are more likely to choose home economics and there is very little difference in biology and history.

What accounts for these marked sex differences in choice? There appear to be three main types of influence at work: differential occupational and career expectations amongst boys and girls, almost exactly reproducing the actual gender-segregated labour market; differential patterns of self and subject attitudes, with girls having less positive subject attitudes and lower educational self-images, particularly in maths and science; and school ethos and teacher support influences which, interacting with the preceding variables, mean that girls require and respond to positive support for unconventional choices to a far greater extent than boys.

Provision/Allocation/Choice

The relative importance of provision, allocation and choice in determining the overall sex differences in rates of subject take-up will, of course, vary depending upon what subject one is analysing. In Table 4 we show three senior-cycle subjects, physics, chemistry and technical drawing. The intention here is to attempt to gauge the relative importance of provision, allocation and choice factors in determining sex differences in take-up. In the case of physics, in our entire Leaving Cert sample 80 per cent of boys as against only 33 per cent of girls were in schools teaching physics. Of that 80 per cent of boys 70 per cent were actually offered physics, as against 58 per cent of the girls in schools where it was taught. This loss of pupils is largely due to their not having met the academic requirements that would allow them to choose physics, in this case because they did not take or obtain a satisfactory result at Inter Cert science. Finally, of those offered the choice of physics, 53 per cent of boys as against 16 per cent of girls actually take it up.

It is clear then that in physics girls are severely disadvantaged, both in the provision of the subject in schools where girls are present and in the allocation of physics to girls where it is on the curriculum. However, the greatest difference between the sexes lies not in provision or allocation but in choice. The same is true of chemistry. Here girls are almost as well provided with the subject as boys. They are at something of a disadvantage in allocation, but the greatest sex difference

111

again occurs in the rates of choice. In technical drawing the situation is a little different. Very few girls are given the choice of this subject and the greatest sex differences arise in allocation where, because they have not done mechanical drawing, girls are virtually all excluded from taking technical drawing. But even of those formally offered it the take-up rate is substantially lower than that of boys. In almost all cases, therefore, changing provision and allocation would only have marginal effects unless the choice rate also goes substantially upwards. Changing this choice rate means intervention to affect girls' self-images, attitudes towards subjects and occupational/career expectations. It also means intervening to change the associated 'hidden curriculum' of teacher and school influences which reinforce conventional roles.

Conclusions
It is clear that very different implicit models of education occur in school decision makers' minds when planning and allocating the curriculum for girls and boys. These school planning agendas are, however, intimately linked with anticipated adult roles that their male and female pupils are likely to play in work, familial and community life. These linked sets of expectations are equally shared by parents and by the majority of pupils themselves. The labour market is so highly gender differentiated that is is hardly surprising that schooling provision and allocation practice has accommodated itself to these adult realities — to clerical, nursing, teaching, other semi-professional jobs, and a very delimited set of industrial and service jobs for females, and a particular conventionalised relationship between the marriage, family, community and labour market roles of women. These packages of roles have become so deeply institutionalised that only the current crisis of dislocation in the labour market could shift the centre of gravity over to less conventional lines. The very fast decline of clerical and office employment and the rapid decline in para-medical and teaching employment, when combined with equally significant changes in the marriage/work-roles of young married women — with over a third of them in their twenties continuing to work after marriage — will force such a shift and provides a unique opportunity for intervention.[8]

8. *Ibid.*, pp 307–10.

It is clear, however, that these conventional expectations are equally shared by pupils themselves and by their parents, with over two-thirds of female pupils aspiring to jobs that are dominantly female in composition and to familial work-roles that are almost equally traditional.[9] So we are dealing with widely shared beliefs concerning female education. These specific sets of conventional expectations, shared by pupils, teachers and parents about adult gender roles, are equalled in significance as determinants of differential subject choice by a more insidious or underground set of educational influences on girls' educational self-images and on their attitudes toward the more difficult and more technical subjects.[10] Girls in general have lower educational self-images, lower confidence in their abilities particularly in maths and science, and more negative views of the usefulness and intrinsic significance of the more 'difficult' subjects. Although girls have in general a more positive view of their educational experience and of their relationship with their teachers and school[11] they have, paradoxically, internalised significantly poorer images of their own performance abilities than have boys even at the same level of actual performance. These 'hidden curricular' influences are in some respects, in fact, more important determinants of differential subject choice than are conventional sex role expectations. Given these circumstances it is not surprising that teachers' support is much more important for girls in pursuing unconventional subject/career choices.

Intervention, if it is to be successful, therefore, cannot be simply concerned with changes in the curriculum or in schools' ways of allocating subjects: it must also concern itself intimately with changing the attitudes, expectations and supportive behaviour of administrators, teachers, pupils and parents. Formal equality of access to a range of subjects would have little impact on differential take-up rates unless it was accompanied by changes in pupils' and teachers' attitudes and expectations. Intervention projects, therefore, are strongly advocated which are designed to bring about positive changes in these directions.[12] But change, if restricted to girls' attitudes, is not enough — there is very clear evidence in our report that female

9. *Ibid.*, p. 72.
10. *Ibid.*, pp 264–76.
11. *Ibid.*, pp 32–48.
12. *Ibid.*, pp 319, 324–9.

pupils and, to some extent, girls' and coeducational schools have changed their attitudes to a far greater extent than have boys' schools or male educational authorities. Changes in conventional male role models are equally necessary — and it appears here that one of the main areas where it is most needed is in the high-achieving middle-class boys' schools. They teach within an extremely conventionalised, narrow educational achievement channel and with expectations of traditional adult gender and parental roles that are more rigid than other schools. Fruitful intervention appears equally necessary here.

Table 1: Sex differences in subject take-up at Inter and Leaving Cert 1980 (selected subjects)

| | Number of candidates | | Ratio of |
	Male	Female	girls/boys
Inter Cert			
Higher maths	7 591	6 552	0.86
Science A	19 422	14 006	0.72
Commerce	11 878	17 775	1.50
Mechanical drawing	10 945	75	0.01
Home economics	107	17 940	167.66
Leaving Cert			
Higher maths	2 461	847	0.34
Physics	4 408	694	0.16
Chemistry	4 524	2 460	0.54
Biology	6 410	12 899	2.01
Applied maths	631	28	0.04
Accounting	3 832	4 823	1.26
Business organisation	4 132	6 143	1.49
Economics	4 750	3 199	0.66
Technical drawing	2 873	17	0.01
Home economics (general)	22	4 538	206.67

Source: Department of Education Statistical Report 1979–80

Table 2: 95 sample schools, Inter Cert science: Type of curricular provision

Science	Not available	Science in core (b)	Science Option or open to all (c)	core to some
Boys' schools (n=24)	0	21	1	2
Girls' schools (n=22)	1	2	12	7
Coed schools (n=49)*	0	30	12	4

*3 coed schools do not have Inter Cert classes this year.
Source: Survey of national sample of post-primary schools, 1981

Table 3: Those pupils choosing the subject as a percentage of those who may choose it (i.e. 'true rate of choice')

Subject	Boys	Girls	Ratio boys/girls
Higher maths	48.7	17.2	2.8
Physics	52.9	16.6	3.2
Chemistry	43.5	27.5	1.6
Biology	49.7	55.6	0.9
History	37.6	33.4	1.1
Technical drawing	56.3	8.9	6.3
Home economics	6.5	44.5	0.1

Source: Hannan and Breen *et al.* 1983, p. 134, Table 5.10.

Table 4: Provision, allocation and choice in physics, chemistry and technical drawing (percentage of Leaving Cert sample)

	Physics		Chemistry		Technical drawing	
	boys	girls	boys	girls	boys	girls
In schools teaching subject:	80	33	80	77	46	17
Of those in schools teaching subject, percentage offered it:	70	58	79	61	58	07
Of those offering it, percentage taking it:	53	16	44	28	56	9

Source: Hannan and Breen *et al.,* 1983, pp 126–7, Table 5.6.

Education for Domestication or Liberation?

Women's involvement in adult education

MARIA SLOWEY

Three-quarters of all women aged twenty to sixty-five are married and, according to official estimates, only eighteen per cent of these married women are engaged in paid employment outside the home.[1] In other words, work for the majority of Irish women means working as a housewife. While this sexual division of labour, where the majority of women work in the home and the vast majority of men are in the paid labour force, represents the dominant feature of modern industrial societies, the situation is even more extreme in Ireland than elsewhere.[2] This sexual division of labour is reproduced through the sexual division of knowledge — that is, the knowledge men and women require to perform their 'appropriate' tasks — and reinforced by the perceptions of and attitudes towards work and education of society and indeed of women themselves.

There is now quite a body of work on how formal education contributes to the traditional division of labour. This is achieved mainly through the structure of the curriculum, where education for girls emphasises arts-based subjects and those geared towards the role of housekeeper, while the curriculum for boys emphasises the 'hard' sciences and technical subjects.[3] Sex-role ideology is reproduced more subtly through the attitudes and expectations of teachers, the sexism of text-

1. Central Statistics Office, *Labour Force Survey, 1979 Results,* Central Statistics Office, Dublin, 1981, Table 8.
2. See for example, Commission of the European Communities, *Women and European Community: Community Action, Comparative National Situations,* Brussels, Commission of the European Communities, 1980.
3. For the current situation in Ireland see D. Hannan *et. al. Schooling and Sex Roles,* E.S.R.I. Publications, Dublin 1983, and, P. Clancy, *Participation in Higher Education,* H.E.A., Dublin, 1982.

books, and the sex bias of counselling and testing procedures.[4] These sources of influence combine not only to channel girls' attitudes and expectations, but also, through educational selection, to severely limit their objective life options. As Sheila Rowbotham puts it:

> This discrimination, masked as 'differentiation' pertains in mixed and segregated schools. It is a combination of attitudes that devalue a girl's achievement, and of a concrete lack of opportunities that undermine it. For in following the trajectory of girls' education one thing, above all, emerges with crystal clarity. It is that there is no coincidence between the natural ability and intelligence of girls and the social devaluation they progressively undergo.[5]

However, what has not been analysed in any systematic way, is the role which education for *adults,* as opposed to education for young people, may play in relation to the position of women generally, and specifically in relation to the sexual division of labour. Every year in Ireland, as in other industrial societies, increasing numbers of women choose to return to some form of educational activity. Can this be seen as potentially a means of redressing the imbalances fostered by their initial cycle of education, or does it in fact simply operate to reinforce the status quo?

To some extent this question can never be answered definitively. The educational system does not operate in a uniform way. It has its own ambiguities and contradictions. Furthermore, while enjoying a relative degree of autonomy, the educational system, as with most institutions in society, is ultimately constrained by the economic system within which it operates.[6] Education can only ameliorate the position of women; of itself it is powerless to effect a real transformation of their situation.

4. For example, N. Glazier-Malbin and M. Y. Waehrer, eds., *Counsellor Bias and the Female Occupational Role,* Chicago, Rand McNally, 1973; G. B. Harrison, *Unlearning the Lie: Sexism in School,* New York, Marrow, 1974; F. Fransella and K. Frost, *On Being a Woman,* London, Tavistock Publications, 1977: C. Adams and R. Laurikietis, *The Gender Trap: I. Education and Work,* London, Virago, 1980.

5. S. Rowbotham, *Women, Resistance and Revolution,* Penguin Books, 1974, p. 40.

6. See Althusser for an interesting analysis of the relationship between education and the economic base. L. Althusser 'Ideology and Ideological State Apparatuses', in *Lenin and Philosophy and Other Essays,* London, New Left Books, 1971.

This qualification should be borne in mind as we examine the current picture of women's involvement in adult education.

Adult education in Ireland

In advanced industrial societies the state has achieved almost total control of formal educational provision, the hierarchical system through which young people are channelled from primary to tertiary level. The provision of education for adults, however, still tends to reflect its very diverse origins in the labour movement, church activities, university extension, women's associations, scientific and literary groups and community activities. This very diversity raises the issue of whether it is in fact possible to refer to an adult education 'system', or whether the reality of the provision is so complex that each part of it must be examined separately.

Unfortunately no general history exists of adult education in Ireland, so all I can do is attempt a very brief overview of the background to the present provision. Direct state involvement in education for adults can be traced to the Agriculture and Technical Institute (Ireland) Act of 1889 which enabled local authorities to levy a rate for vocational education. The Vocational Education Act of 1930 established thirty-eight Vocational Education Committees (VECs), which were obliged to provide for the educational needs of adults in their areas. This provision in practice extended far beyond vocational courses to embrace a wide variety of subject areas defined as being of a 'recreational' nature. Most of these classes took place in school premises in the evening, and have come to account for the largest number of adults involved in taking courses. Community and comprehensive schools, established in the 1970s, have continued and developed this tradition.

The other main forms of direct involvement by the state in adult education are through AnCO — The Industrial Training Authority — and, for workers in agriculture, through ACOT. Shortly before the establishment of AnCO, a document published by the Organisation for Economic Co-Operation and Development stated in relation to Ireland that there was 'no general adult education programme in Ireland and no manpower retraining programme in particular'.[7] This sector of adult education has in fact expanded rapidly since then,

7. OECD, *Review of National Policies for Education: Ireland,* Paris, OECD, 1969, p. 81.

because training is explicitly linked to the economy, because there is an international emphasis on the necessity for training and retraining in times of rapid technological change, and because of financial support from Europe. While most women trainees continue to be trained for the traditional female sectors of the labour force, AnCO has been involved in some innovative (if often threatened) work for women — such as the return to work courses of the 1970s and the support for women's co-operatives in the 1980s.

The universities have been involved in adult education through their extra-mural departments, which generally provide courses of a liberal–academic character. Unlike Britain where the universities work closely with the Workers' Education Association, attempts by the Irish universities to provide workers' education have generally not been very successful. The trade unions themselves (besides their internal education programmes) sponsor, through the Irish Congress of Trade Unions, courses directly related to trade union activities, and, through the People's College, courses of a more general character.

Adult education in Ireland is remarkable for the degree of involvement by the Catholic church. This occurs directly, through various adult education institutes (eg the College of Industrial Relations and the Dublin Institute of Adult Education) and indirectly, through its involvement in a great many 'community-based' activities.

Besides these main sources, there is a myriad of voluntary groups (including political groups) who sponsor educational activities of many kinds. One most interesting development was the establishment of a short-term residential college for women (An Grianán) by the Irish Country Women's Association. While the emphasis here has always been on liberal studies and crafts, recently more vocationally orientated courses have been provided. Apart from the educational content of these courses, they represented a significant step for many married women, who were often staying away from their husband and family for the first time.

In contrast to these forms of adult education, where the initiative and control lay to a greater or lesser extent with the providing body, the early 1980s saw the emergence of self-directed adult education groups. These groups were essentially community-based and focused particularly on the educational needs of women. Their origins can be traced to a combination of two very important developments. Firstly, there was the consciousness-raising and self-help approach adopted by the women's movement in the previous decade. This approach placed the key emphasis on the recognition of the experiences of women, taking as a starting point women's own definition of their needs. Simultaneously with these developments some of those involved in adult education were being influenced by the ideas of Paolo Friere, who emphasised the importance of non-formal educational activities and recognition of the social context in which the participants lived.[8]

The study of women in adult education on which this paper is based was undertaken in the late 1970s and therefore pre-dates many of these latter developments. The fact remains however, that the great majority of women participating in adult education continue to attend 'mainstream' courses of the kind provided through the VEC system, extra-mural university departments, adult education institutes and training bodies. Like the respondents in the study they still face conflicting expectations and choices about being mothers and wives as well as being independent adults with their own intellectual, creative, social and economic lives.

Background to the study
With the objective of exploring the patterns of women's participation in adult education, and women's own views of the role adult education could play for them, a study was undertaken over the period 1977 and 1978. While some changes in the pattern of women's involvement in adult education have taken place since then, the fundamental position of married women in Irish society has remained much the same, as have the issues raised by the women in the survey. This involved in-depth interviews with 126 married women in the Dublin area who had recently attended some form of adult education. The focus was on courses which involved some form of registration, but which required either no formal entry qualifications or minimal level requirements.

Because of the qualitative nature of the study, the very complex nature of adult education provision and the absence of any overall statistics, it was not possible to devise a strict random

8. P. Friere, *Pedagogy of the Oppressed,* Penguin.

sample. An approximation was achieved by purposely select-ing examples of the main providers of the types of adult educa-tion being considered, and then randomly selecting from these agencies a sample of women who had attended their courses. Thus, of the 126 women who were interviewed, approximately 48 per cent had attended courses in evening schools, 24 per cent in industrial training centres, 14 per cent in a university extra-mural department, 9 per cent in adult education institutes, and the remainder in community centres. Unfortunately, there are not national records available to show how accurately this reflects the actual distribution. Some support for its representativeness comes from the fact that in another large scale study 42 per cent of all courses attended by adults in Dublin were provided through evening schools.[9]

In Ireland, as in other western societies, it is the men and women who have already enjoyed a relatively high level of formal education who are the most likely to participate in further educational activities as adults.[10] A comprehensive random sample of the Dublin area showed that whereas two-thirds of those who had never participated in adult education had left school under the age of fifteen, only one-third of those who had participated in adult education had left at that age.[11] At the other end of the scale, those who stayed in formal educa-tion beyond the age of eighteen were almost three times as likely to have been adult education participants.

The sexual division of knowledge

Two recent Irish studies by Hannan and Clancy have supple-mented earlier work by the Commission on the Status of Women in providing clear evidence of the sexual division of

9. Obtained by secondary analysis of data generously made available by Michael McGréil to the author. For a full report on the survey see M. McGréil, *Prejudice and Tolerance in Ireland,* Dublin, College of Industrial Relations, 1977.

10. The largest scale study still remains that of J. W. C. Johnstone and R. J. Rivera, *Volunteers for Learning: A Study of the Educational Pursuits of American Adults,* Chicago, Aldine, 1965. In Britain the report of a national survey of adults in education is due for publication in early 1987. A. Woodley, L. Wagner, M. Slowey, M. Hamilton, O. Fulton *Choosing to Learn: A National Survey of Adults in Education.* Open University Press.

11. McGréil op. cit.

knowledge, which exists in the formal educational system. They show how women are consistently under-represented in vocationally orientated technical and scientific subjects and over-represented in arts, languages and social sciences. Mainly because of the 'marginal' nature of adult education, but also on account of its decentralised form of provision, no comparable figures are available, even in unpublished form, for the sexual division of knowledge within the adult education sphere. So in order to obtain some indication of the situation within adult education, the records of a number of institutions representing the main providers of adult education courses were examined.[13] Because of the small scale of the enquiry, it must be emphasised that these figures must be taken as suggestive only. They do, however, indicate how the traditional sexual division of knowledge is reproduced in the adult education sphere.

In Table 1, three main adult education course areas are identified: familial-home courses, which cover subjects such as cookery, sewing, child-care etc; creative–conceptual courses, which cover subjects such as crafts, hobbies and the humanities; and work-related courses, which cover vocational and trade union courses. There is a clear divide between vocational and non-vocational courses — whereas women represented approximately three-quarters of the participants on non-vocational courses, men represented over eighty per cent of the participants on vocational courses. While the proportion of women on vocational courses has increased somewhat in recent years, the pattern for non-vocational courses has remained much the same. Data from a recent large-scale study on mature students in England and Wales is provided for

12. Op. cit.
13. The enrolment records of representatives of the four main types of institutions to be covered in the sample were examined. The institutions were an extra-mural department, five night schools (VEC), an adult education centre with an emphasis on industrial relations and industrial training centres. Obtaining figures for night schools gave severe practical problems as no central data were available on a sex breakdown by type of course. In this case it was necessary to go through the roll books of a sample of schools, and deduce sex by people's names. Where a name was not sex-specific (e.g. Pat) or where initials only were given, the person was omitted.

comparative purposes.[14] It is apparent that non-qualifying courses (which are almost exclusively non-vocational) are attended largely by women, while qualifying courses (which are generally more vocational in orientation) are more likely to be attended by men.

Table 1: Sex distribution across types of course in selected institutions in Ireland, England and Wales (percentages)

SEX	Ireland[a]			England and Wales[b]	
	Non-Vocational		Vocational	Non-Qualifying	Qualifying
	Familial –home	Creative –conceptual			
Female	86	71	17	77	46
Male	14	29	83	23	54

(a) Based on an examination of the records of industrial training centres, an adult education centre, an extra-mural department and a sample of five night schools — see note 13 for details.

(b) Based on a random sample of mature students in all forms of education — see note 14 for details.

It is interesting to look more closely at the familial–home types of course for two reasons — firstly, because they are attended almost exclusively by women and are obviously related to the social role of 'housewife', and secondly, because they constitute such a large proportion of all courses attended by women. Many of the important works on women in the 1960s focused on the nature of the role of housewife as a key aspect of women's oppression.[15] Later studies attempted to place the role of housewife within the context of occupational sociology by identifying the differences and similarities between the role of housewife and any other form of work.[16]

14. Based on data from the Mature Students Research Project, a large-scale study of mature students in England and Wales undertaken for the Department of Education and Science by a consortium of the Polytechnic of Central London, the Open University and Lancaster University over the period 1980–3. See Woodley et al., opate.

15. For example, B. Friedan, *The Feminine Mystique,* Penguin, 1963; M. Gavron, *The Captive Wife,* Penguin, 1966.

16. For example, M. Z. Lopata, *Occupation Housewife,* Oxford University Press, New York, 1971. A. Oakley, *The Sociology of Housework,* Martin Robertson, London, 1977.

One of the many differences identified was that the job of housewife was one for which there were no selection procedures and no training — unlike any other work the job is performed by a representative cross-section of the entire married female population regardless of class, background or education.

Until this century it was assumed that the skills required by women for the reproduction of the labour force through the family unit in terms of food preparation, housekeeping, child-rearing and sexual services, would be learnt through informal socialisation from their mothers and other female relatives by young women. More recently, while the roles of wife, mother and housekeeper may still be regarded as 'natural' for women, it is no longer automatically assumed that women will have learnt all the necessary skills for their performance. One of the rationales for the necessity of courses on domestic subjects and child-rearing lies in the diminishing opportunities for informal learning due to the break-up of the extended family. A further reason is what is regarded as the increasing complexity of running a home in times of rapid social and technological change. Oakley's book *Housewife,* a review of international studies on housework from the 1920s up to the 1970s, shows that the amount of time spent on housework (an average of seventy-seven hours per week in 1971 in Britain) showed no tendency to decrease over time.[17]

The problem of distinguishing the ideological component from the skill component in any form of education and training is always a difficult one. This is particularly the case in relation to training for the unique role of housewife. Courses in housework and related subjects can be seen as representing attempts to raise the status of such areas into subjects in their own right. As Schlossman points out in his work on the origin of family education in the United States: 'Formal training in the household chores it was argued, would make women content as housewives by teaching them the challenges hidden within traditional responsibilities.'[18]

How does involvement in formal education affect women's choice of course? It might be expected that the women who had undergone the longest socialisation within the formal educa-

17. A. Oakley, *Housewife,* Penguin, 1976, p. 7.
18. S. L. Schlossman, 'Before Homestart', *Harvard Educational Review,* (Vol. 46, No. 3, 1976), p. 447.

tional system would be the most likely to select the creative–conceptual types of course, firstly because their involvement in an educational system heavily geared towards the arts would have alerted them to the 'superiority' of creative–conceptual types of content and, secondly, because they would be more likely to be familiar with these areas of knowledge, which are rather esoteric and not part of the stock of everyday knowledge.[19] On the other hand, it would seem likely that women with a relatively low formal educational background would be most heavily represented within the home–familial content areas which deal with everyday knowledge. Being less familiar with the idea of going to a course in the first place, it seems that if women in this group do participate in adult education, they would be likely to select a subject area which is relevant to their sphere of activity, which for many would mean their duties in the home. Thus, for example, courses in cookery would probably appear as more accessible to women with a low educational background than courses in subjects such as archaeology or sociology.

Support for these suppositions comes from the major studies in Britain and the US. Unfortunately, the former does not provide a breakdown by sex but it is pointed out that

> Subjects grouped as 'academic', 'liberal', 'arts', or 'languages' all attract people with distinctively higher TEAs [Terminal Educational Ages] and social class ratings — it is in relation to these types of courses that the discrepancy in representation of different education and social groups is at a maximum.[20]

The patterns of participation in the American study showed a direct relationship between level of education and attendance at conceptual-creative courses with 42 per cent of women who had a college education attending these types of courses as opposed to 31 per cent of those with a high school education and only 17 per cent of those with a grade school education. On

---

19. Some interesting work has been done on the influence of education on other aspects of cultural consumption, namely the 'arts' and 'high culture', see P. Diamaggio and M. Useem 'Social Class and Arts Consumption', *Theory and Society*, (Vol. 5, 1978); P. Bourdieu, 'Outline of a Sociological Theory of Arts Perceptions', *International Social Science Journal* (Vol. 20, 1968).
20. Johnstone and Rivera, *op. cit.*, p. 107.

the other hand, there was an inverse relationship between level of education and attendance at familial courses — 14 per cent of college educated women attended this type of course as opposed to 20 per cent of high school women and 24 per cent of grade school women.

In order to explore this point, the courses attended by women in my survey were grouped into four broad categories — familial–home, vocational, creative–conceptual and community orientated. Table 2 shows the educational background of respondents attending these different types of course. It is clear that women who stayed longest within the formal education system were most likely to have attended creative–conceptual courses, while women who left school at a relatively early age were most likely to have attended familial–home courses. Thus the group with the latest school-leaving age were over twice as likely to have attended creative–conceptual courses as the earliest school-leaving group, with the middle educational group occupying an intermediary position. The situation is even more pronounced for the familial–home courses, which accounted for the type of course attended by 42 per cent of all the women who left school aged fifteen or under. These early school leavers were *seven* times as likely to have attended this type of course as the latest school-leaving group, and were also twice as likely as the intermediary group to have attended familial–home courses. The same pattern was revealed by the other measure of educational attainment — highest qualification obtained. Notably, no woman who had received a university qualification attended a familial–home course, but on the other hand, two-thirds of them had attended creative–conceptual courses.

Table 2. Type of course attended by respondents by age finishing full-time education (percentages)

Type of course	15 or under	16–17	Over 17
Familial–home	42	20	6
Vocational	26	23	28
Community	17	28	31
Creative–conceptual	15	29	34
Total N	43	50	33

Although it appears that the higher the level of formal education a women has the more likely she is to participate in community courses, the relationship does not seem to be as strong as with the previous two types of course. Also, women from each educational group were almost equally likely to have attended vocational courses. It must be borne in mind that the sample was stratified to yield fairly equal representation from each type of course, and that in the actual population of adult students only a very small minority of women are at present taking these types of course. While it is dangerous to generalise without more information on the levels of the courses being taken by the women and the type of work for which they are being prepared, it does seem that an expansion of the opportunities for vocational courses for women might contribute to some reduction in the social inequalities that exist between women of different educational backgrounds, as well as leading to greater participation by women in the labour force.

Women's view of adult education

How do women themselves view their involvement in these activities? In particular, what about the processes by which they decided to take part in different courses, and what overall role do they see adult education playing in their lives?

An attempt was made in this study to overcome some of the defects of previous research dealing with the issue of why people choose to attend adult education activities. Most of these studies employed highly structured questionnaires which exercise a strong channelling influence on people's response.[21] Instead, I sought to develop a dynamic approach to motivation, which would allow the respondents to use their own vocabulary in describing their reasons for participating in adult education, and which would place these responses within the context of their lives. Two basic assumptions underlay the conception of motivation used in this study: firstly, that motives are socially produced; secondly, that motivation is never a single entity but is multidimensional.

21. One review of this research concluded that so far 'it has neither yielded new points of enquiry, confirmed uncertain findings, nor developed new methods. In fact, the investigations which deal with participation in adult education have been of strikingly little inter-disciplinary importance'. K. Rubenson, *Recruitment in Adult Education: A Research Strategy*, Sweden, Stockholm School of Education, 1976.

The vocabulary of motivation

The work of C.W. Mills is helpful in understanding the social nature of motivation:

> Motives are generally thought of as subjective 'springs' of action lying in the psychic structure or organism of the individual. But there is another way to think of them. Since persons ascribe motives to themselves and to other persons we may consider motives as the terms which persons typically use in their interpersonal relations.'[22]

In other words, the way motives are expressed is determined to a large extent by an available vocabulary which is deemed to adequately describe some action within a particular social context. The most important effect of the social character of motives is that different motives are available for use by people in different structural (eg class, race, sex, age) positions. Furthermore, if the individual does not explicitly express a motive, other people will use this vocabulary to ascribe motives to them. Thus, for example, it has generally been regarded as appropriate that men should express a strong, if not aggressive, career motivation, while the same motivation has been regarded as inappropriate, or even 'unnatural', if expressed by women. This process is self-reinforcing: 'The approved motives which are typically ascribed to conduct are sanctions which reinforce that conduct. Disapproved motives are sanctions which discourage the conduct to which they are typically applied.'[23]

A problem of social legitimation can arise, therefore, when a group of people find themselves without a vocabulary with which to give expression to some particular situation. Becker, in a study of depression amongst married women, suggests that part of the surrender to despair and feelings of self-deprecation associated with depression, is due to the fact that the individual finds herself in a difficult situation which she is unable to define, in other words a situation for which she has no adequate vocabulary. The vocabulary of guilt therefore serves

22. H. Gerth and C.W. Mills, *Character and Social Structure,* London, Routledge and Kegan Paul, 1970, pp. 114-115.
23. *Ibid.,* p.128.

'as the perfect justification for failure where this failure cannot be otherwise understood'.[24]

In exploring how respondents to my questionnaire expressed their motivation for participating in adult education activities, I was trying to find out the vocabulary which seemed to them to be appropriate for describing married women's attendance at courses. From a detailed analysis of the answers to open-ended questions relating directly to this topic, as well as a content analysis of the total interview, it seems that a new orthodoxy is emerging as to what constitute legitimate vocabularies of motives for married women.

While the analysis supported the view that motivation must be viewed as complex and multidimensional, a central element did emerge which was clearly related to the structural situation of married women and the range of options open to them. It appears that the position of women working in the home leads them to adopt an almost dichotomous view of the world, with the home representing the point of division. In her classic work Lopata develops this idea of an 'inside–outside' continuum. She suggests that for the housewife:

> The stress upon the location of the self 'inside' the home as opposed to 'outside' life, roles or persons ... begins with a gradual shift of the image of the self from a rather functionally diffused 'outside' existence, to a role focused and geographically placed identity within the home.[25]

Almost 80 per cent of the women surveyed spontaneously explained their participation in terms of this issue: thus 57 per cent of respondents used a vocabulary of wishing to pursue an interest 'outside' the home to describe this important aspect of their participation, while on the other hand some 20 per cent said they wished to pursue an interest 'inside' the home. Eleven per cent gave more general reasons: they wanted 'to do something' or had 'time available'. Eight per cent said they 'wanted to get involved', 'to get into circulation', responses which, although again deriving from the structural situation of housewives, seemed to involve a more active dimension than simply a

24. E. Becker, "Mills' Social Psychology and the Great Historical Convergence on the Problem of Alienation", in I.L. Horowitz, ed., *The New Sociology,* New York, Oxford University Press, 1964.
25. Lopata op. cit.

desire to do 'something' outside the home. Only 4 per cent did not express their motivation in these or related terms.

These results support the argument that while the world of the family and the home is still seen as the main focus of women's lives, there has been a growing recognition that this arena alone cannot satisfy all their needs all the time. What is required therefore to maintain the status quo is a vocabulary which assists women in developing motivations to undertake activities in other spheres of social life, but which will be unlikely to pose a fundamental threat to the ultimate primacy of their roles as mother, wife and housekeeper. I call this vocabulary the 'vocabulary of interests'.

The function of the vocabulary of interests is to provide married women with a socially legitimate rationale for participating in activities in spheres other than the home and family. When a woman says she is doing something 'just for an interest', she is reaffirming that the activity does not conflict with her commitment to her main duties. This vocabulary of motive can lead to participation in a wide variety of activities — for example hobbies, voluntary work, education, etc, and it can even be used in relation to participation in the labour market. Married women are the only section of the population who have to justify their wish to engage in paid employment. Particularly in times of high male unemployment, and in Irish society where the traditional sex-role ideology remains very strong, married women sometimes incur severe social sanctions for working outside the home. One way in which they can attempt to legitimate undertaking paid employment (when not in 'extreme' financial need) is by explaining their motivation as 'working for an interest outside the home'. The use of this terminology emphasises that employment poses no real threat to their primary obligations, in a way which the use of another vocabulary (eg that of pursuits of ambition, independence, status, money) might do.

Role of adult education

Adult education can play several roles for individuals at different times and in different circumstances. I attempted to discover the dominant meaning which respondents felt it had for them. For a given individual it is an ahistorical 'snapshot' at the time of the interview. From this analysis it appeared that adult education plays four principal roles for these women —

firstly, it provides a source of contact and sense of social involvement; secondly, it is a means of learning more about particular subjects of interest to the respondents; thirdly, they see it as a means of improving their general knowledge and level of education; finally, it provides them with some external means of assessing their own skills and abilities.

Almost one-third of the respondents (30 per cent) saw adult education mainly as a means of social involvement and social contact. For these women adult education provides a link between the confines of the home and the wider community. Reflecting the isolation of housewives, some of them place the emphasis on the opportunity for a sharing of interests and meaningful interaction with other adults:

At classes I've a chance to talk about things outside the home. I've different conversations than normally.

Classes are important to me because I meet people I can talk to instead of talking at the kids' level all day.

Courses pass the time and are interesting.

The content of the courses does not tend to be as important for these women as the chance such activities offer to have more serious conversations than their ordinary daily interaction provides for them. Other women, who saw the role of adult education in terms of social involvement, put more stress on the opportunity it provides for a break in their routine, and simply as an enjoyable outlet for them:

I would go to the tech to meet people even if I never learnt anything. I enjoy a bit of crack.

I enjoy it. I look forward to going to classes as a night out.

I get bored occasionally, that's why I go to classes.

In contrast to this group the content of the courses was the most important factor for approximately a quarter of respondents (26 per cent). These women saw adult education as a way of acquiring particular knowledge and skills. This represents an instrumental view of adult education where it is seen as a useful means of achieving particular goals:

Classes aren't a means of getting out for me as I have lots of other interests. I go because I want to learn about a particular subject.

I've done all work related courses. Adult classes train me for the job I want.

I only went to the course to learn cookery. I have nothing to do with adult education or education in general.

Reading is not enough for me when I want to learn about something so I go to the classes.

Approximately the same proportion of the sample (25 per cent) viewed adult education as a source of learning opportunities and a means of generally improving their education. Sometimes there was a deeper overlap between this meaning and the social involvement meaning, as women would see adult education as an activity which provides an opportunity to meet people as well as a chance to learn something. In most cases it was possible, however, to identify which role was uppermost for the respondents:

Classes mean education and bettering myself, and are also an outside interest.

I always regret I never had a degree and I want to try and make up for it.

I like to educate myself. To keep my mind alert.

A particularly interesting finding was that about 15 per cent of the women saw adult education activities as principally providing an important means through which they could not only use, but also *assess* their skills and abilities. This need would relate to certain features of the role of housewife. 'Housewives', as Oakley points out, 'are impressed by their freedom from the constraints of externally set rules and supervisors. However, a consequence of this autonomy is their responsibility for seeing that housework gets done. The housewife is her own supervisor, the judge of her own performance, and ultimately the source of her own job definition.' Some of the elements of a satisfying job are challenge and autonomy,

132

coupled with some form of external validation. In this situation the individual has an opportunity of both using her skill and initiative and, through feedback, to obtain some idea of how good her performance is. Conventionally the only time a housewife's work is noticed is when it has not been done. Educational activities thus provide situations where an individual can set her own goals and obtain an external indication of how well she meets them. For most of the women this feedback is positive:

I had a dread of going to classes because the nuns were dreadful to me at school ... but in fact going to them showed me I was able to learn.

I discover things about myself I didn't know – hidden talents.

Some of the classes are beyond me, but I enjoy trying them anyway.

Summary and conclusion
In this paper an attempt has been made to analyse the role which adult education may be playing for Irish women at the moment. We saw how, as in other western societies, the women who attend adult education activities tend to have already had a relatively good educational background compared to the population of women as a whole. In spite of this, however, a substantial minority of the respondents had left school by the age of fifteen with no educational qualifications. Whether this constitutes a genuine 'second chance' depends to a large extent on the types of course they take, and as, was shown, they tended to be over-represented in the traditionally female areas of familial–home courses. Whether these courses actually transmit skills which are necessary to the successful fulfilment of the social role of housewife, or whether they have an entirely ideological function, the fact remains that they operate to reinforce the traditional position of women in the home.

In looking at how the respondents expressed their reasons for participating in adult education activities it was suggested that the most fruitful approach was to regard motives a vocabularies which are supplied through ideology. As the traditional ideology of women's role is still dominant in Irish society, it is not surprising that most of the women in the survey that the most fruitful approach was to regard motives as

133

chose to express their motives in terms which are defined in terms of their home and family, and their roles as wife, mother and housekeeper. Furthermore, when the context of their decision to participate is explored, the vast majority of respondents replied in terms of a desire to 'pursue an interest' either inside or outside the home. The argument is made here that while on the face of it this may seem like a move away from the traditional primacy of the family and home as the source of all a woman's satisfactions, it could also have the effect of sustaining the status quo in the face of mounting pressure for real change. In other words, a new conventional wisdom has developed which recognises the 'need' for women to have other interests besides the home–family nexus, but which at the same time has the effect of deflecting any real moves for change into an outlet which, as presently constituted, is unlikely to threaten the existing structural relationships between the sexes.

Education has always been looked to by social reformers as a way of achieving some degree of social change. As the final section of this paper showed, participation in adult education was of some considerable personal importance for quite a large section of the respondents. It increased their confidence and gave them an opportunity to develop and assess their abilities. Obviously these are important steps in any moves towards sexual equality, providing women with essential intellectual and social stimulation and an opportunity to see themselves as individuals rather than appendages to their families. The question remains, however, as to whether adult education in its present form provides the best way of assisting these women to translate their vague wishes to 'get involved' and their growing feelings of confidence, into the more material gains of participation within the wider economic, social and political spheres. The evidence of this study suggests that there is a danger that this is not the case, and that going to a class can become an end in itself, thus probably defusing the momentum for change. However there seems to be two important exceptions to this dominant pattern. Firstly, if women shifted their attendance from familial–home and liberal studies to attendance at courses which lead either to a particular vocational skill or an educational qualification, then they would be in a realistic position to re-enter the work force, which is a minimum prerequisite to redressing sexual inequalities.

The second area of possible change comes from the rapid

increase over the past few years of new forms of self-directed adult education activities for women, which either directly or indirectly are geared towards challenging the traditional position of women. These activities take many forms, including informal women's discussion groups, courses on a variety of topics which are organised to suit the routine and needs of women with domestic responsibilities, and women's studies courses which in a more explicit way take as their subject matter the examination of the position of women in society. These are exciting developments and it will be interesting in the future to examine the effects of such activities on those who participate in them. There will, of course, be great difficulties, not only because many women remain untouched by them, but also because the heavy emphasis on the humanities and social sciences still makes it very difficult for women to break into non-traditional areas of work.

This paper is based on research funded through an Aontas–Carrolls Research Fellowship 1976–1979. The views expressed are those of the author.

Knowledge and Power: patriarchal knowledge on the feminist curriculum

MARY CULLEN

S tereotypes of femininity have changed over time and so has the education available to women. The current stereotype of femininity does not explicitly insist that women are by nature intellectually and morally inferior to men, as previous models, such as those of Aristotle and Thomas Aquinas, have regularly done. Current educational provision for girls allows them, in theory if not always in practice, access to more or less the same subjects as boys. But the core of the stereotype and the essential nature of the differences in the educational experience of the two sexes have undergone little change.

The current version of the stereotypes of what it is to be a woman says that women, all of them or most of them, are best fufilled personally as individual human beings and make their best contribution to society by a life as wife and mother full-time in the home. This model influences the educational experience of girls and women in a number of ways. It determines the areas of human knowledge made available to and seen as suitable for girls and women. It affects the encouragement and discouragement given to girls to study various subjects. It influences the choices girls themselves make and the degrees of self-confidence they bring to the subjects chosen.

The problem feminism sees with the stereotype is that it is based on a narrow, functionalist definition of women's nature. Women as a group are assigned a strictly defined and limited role in society, that of wife and mother full-time in the home. Being a wife and mother is expanded into a vocation that should occupy a woman's time and energy to the exclusion of serious commitment to the development of other talents or to other forms of contribution to society. The characteristics and abilities that are judged to fit women to carry out the role of wife and mother as it is thus socially constructed are then defined as 'feminine' and as rooted in women's nature. However, their being natural is not deemed to be sufficient and the nurturing and development of these characteristics is declared to be the most important objective in the education of females. The end result is that the training of a wife and mother to fit the

136

stereotype takes precedence over what should be the primary purpose, the drawing out of the full potential of the individual human person.

The patriarchal paradigm of male–female relationships which produces this feminine stereotype also produces a complementary masculine model. Western patriarchal thinking has always seen the male as the human norm and has always constructed the role and nature of the female in relation to his perceived needs. Today's stereotypical male, active, dominant, competitive and aggressive, is well served by a passive, subordinate, self-effacing, nurturing female. *He* manages the world and *she* remains in the home to nurture him and the next generation who in turn will fit into the same pattern. Each stereotype encourages the exaggerated development of one set of characteristics, some desirable for all human beings and some desirable for none, and the underdevelopment of others. The feminine stereotype in particular cuts off wide areas of activity and experience as inappropriate for women, and these tend to be the areas most highly prized and rewarded. That the feminine stereotype is in reality rated as less valuable and desirable, whatever the lip service to the contrary, is revealed in the essential difference in the taboos for either sex on behaviour associated with the opposite stereotype. The insult to masculinity in the accusation of 'acting like a woman' is quite different in kind to the insult to femininity in the reverse accusation.

Feminism sees both stereotypes as less than fully human. Neither can be seen as the model of a rounded, adult human person and to attempt to conform to either is to risk never achieving responsible maturity. In so far as the experience of girls and boys within formal educational systems teaches them to become women and men as defined by the patriarchal stereotypes, feminism cannot accept the current education of either sex as non-sexist or fully human.

Feminists have always seen education as one of the key areas where the patriarchal values of the dominant group in society are reinforced and passed on. Feminist strategies for eliminating sexism in education are most often aimed at the hidden curriculum of attitudes and expectations which students, teachers, parents and society in general bring to the education of girls and boys. These are rightly seen to be powerful influences on the educational experience of both sexes. However, it seems to me that there are pitfalls associated with the development of such strategies and that they need to be carefully thought through in the context of what the ultimate objective is intended to be.

There are two implicit premises underlying strategies aimed at the hidden curriculum. The first is that girls are disadvantaged relative to boys by reason of a conditioning process that puts them at a disadvantage in the encounter with the content of what they study, particularly in relation to areas regarded as 'boys' subjects'. The second premise is that, if girls were not inhibited by stereotypes of what sort of knowledge is suitable for them, or by fears that, by reason of their sex, they were less likely than boys to succeed at some or all subjects, they would than start on equal terms with boys and share a similar educational experience.

If both premises are accepted as true, what conclusions follow? Encouraging girls to study 'boys' subjects' and to adopt similar career paths, and bolstering their confidence in their ability to do so, certainly confront issues of discrimination and the distribution of resources and power in society, and it is important that these be tackled. But there is a danger that these strategies may sometimes, in practice if not in theory, narrow into concentration on gaining for girls equal opportunity to compete for the glittering prizes of economic and social power. It is questionable if this is the best best way to draw out full human potential. Also, if the education of boys does in any way contribute to the creation of the patriarchal male, caution seems called for in seeking a similar experience for girls.

Even when the ultimate objective is seen as a more fundamental renegotiation of roles between the sexes a major problem remains. This is that the second premise does not stand up under scrutiny. Strategies aimed at changing the hidden curriculum, however successful they may be, cannot by themselves give girls and boys a similar educational experience. Sexism in education does not derive solely from the sexist attitudes we bring to it. If it did the implication would be that the actual knowledge taught and learned transcends sex and gender and is equally 'female' and 'male'. Unfortunately this is not the case. The content of what is studied also needs to be taken into account.

A growing body of feminist studies has established that the

actual subject matter studied, the body of knowledge and theory passed on as our western intellectual inheritance both within and without the formal educational system, is for the most part permeated with patriarchal values. Because this is so, and because this knowledge and theory is presented as 'human' and its patriarchal nature either trivialised or effectively rendered invisible, the encounter with it cannot provide the same experience for females and for males. The overt as well as the hidden curriculum is permeated by patriarchal values and powerfully transmits and reinforces these.

The creation and validation of knowledge has been a central focus of feminist studies. The starting point is the axiom that knowledge is not and cannot be value-free. It is a human construct brought into being by the interaction of the human mind with its environment. It reflects the experience and values of the individuals and groups who create it. The knowledge and theory passed on as our intellectual inheritance are for the most part based on the male experience and constructed within the framework of a patriarchal paradigm of human society. They consistently see the male as the human norm and as the active agent in the activities which they rank as the highest human achievements, intellectual and artistic creativity, political, economic and social leadership and dominance. They consistently see women as relative to men, define them in terms of how they serve male needs, and seldom perceive them as autonomous human persons in their own right.

Some examples of feminist critical analysis will give an indication of the nature of the contribution of feminist scholarship to the analysis of patriarchy. Its implications for the development of strategies for non-sexist education will then be considered.

The first example is taken from two studies of the relation between Aristotle's *Biology* and his *Politics*. Lynda Lange[1] points out that the views of Aristotle and other philosophers as to the essential differences between the human nature of women and men are usually treated by twentieth-century scholars as unimportant and irrelevant to the main body of

1. Lynda Lange, 'Women is not a rational animal: on Aristotle's biology of reproduction', in Sandra Harding and Merrill B. Hintikka, *Discovering Reality; feminist perspectives on epistemology, meta-physics, methodology, and philosophy of science,* D. Reidel Publishing Company, Holland/Boston 1983, pp 1–16.

thought of the philosopher in question. She argues that this treatment results in a distortion of that 'main' work. In his *Biology*, Aristotle sets out his proof that women are not rational animals in the way that men are. This is his basic justification for excluding women from citizenship in the *Politics*. The non-citizenship of women in the *Politics* is a natural result of their non-rationality in the *Biology*. Aristotle himself, she points out, recognised the link when he said that consideration of the nature of things is a basic starting point in political philosophy.

Elizabeth V. Spelman[2] looks at the implications of Aristotle's denial of the full rationality of women for the internal consistency of his argument and finds that it leads to serious internal flaws in the logical development of the latter. He justifies male authority over women by analogy with the argument that in the human soul there is a rational and an irrational element and that it is natural for the rational element to have authority over the irrational. So, he argues, men should have authority over women because in women the rational element in the human soul is easily overruled by the irrational. Spelman points out that what Aristotle is actually saying is that it is natural for women to be in what he himself has declared to be an unnatural state, that is, one in which the irrational overrules the rational. To reach the desired justification of male authority Aristotle contradicts one of his own basic premises.

The second example is the use of the adversary or adversarial paradigm in the methodology of philosophical debate. Janice Moulton[3] defines the adversary paradigm as the belief that philosophical enquiry is most effectively advanced by subjecting a philosophical theory to the severest possible criticism. Within this paradigm the presentation of a piece of work often takes the form of imagining counter-arguments and seeking to refute them. Moulton points to two serious problems associated with the adversary paradigm. The first is that the adversarial method is more easily adopted by men than by women because the patriarchal stereotypes see aggressive behaviour as relatively less culpable in men than in women. In some cases they even see it as positively praiseworthy in males

2. Elizabeth V. Spelman, 'Aristotle and the politicization of the soul', *ibid.*, pp 17–30.
3. Janice Moulton, 'A paradigm of philosophy: the adversary method', *ibid.*, pp 149–64.

while they are consistently more disapproving in their attitude towards female aggression. Women, she argues, will be more likely to feel inhibited in adopting methods of evaluation by all-out attack while men will feel less so or not inhibited at all. This situation puts women immediately at a disadvantage relative to men in the development of philosophical theory in situations where this methodology is used.

Moulton's second criticism is that she sees weaknesses in the adversary paradigm as a method for advancing knowledge, which is of course its primary purpose and justification. The method concentrates activity on isolating the weak links in a chain of argument and seeking to undermine these. The result, she argues, is to distract attention from the proposed theory as a whole and to encourage the proposer of it to concentrate on counter-attacking on individual points that may not be important to the main argument. It also inhibits the critic from putting forward alternative systems of ideas based on different premises and different data.

The third example is taken from the growing body of feminist analysis of the development of modern science from the period of the scientific revolution of the sixteenth and seventeenth centuries. In *Science and Sexual Aggression*[4] Brian Easlea argues that the movement explicitly incorporated patriarchal values as part of itself. The natural philosophers of the revolution described their science as 'hard' and 'masculine'. Women were not capable of serious involvement because of their 'softness', by which they meant literal softness of brain fibre. Objectives and methods were explained in similarly patriarchal language. Science would pursue knowledge by forcing nature to reveal 'her' secrets, by 'penetrating' 'her' womb' and by subduing a 'feminine' nature by 'masculine' human power.

Easlea sees a causal link between the sexism of the natural philosophers and the irrational aggression of their approach to nature and science. He draws on the work of feminist sociology

4. Brian Easlea, *Science and sexual aggression; patriarchy's confrontation with women and nature,* Weidenfeld and Nicolson, London 1981.

and psychoanalysis, and notably that of Nancy Chodorow,[5] in looking for explanations for the origins of patriarchy. Following this work, he theorises that the root cause of both aggressions is to be found in the problems males face in establishing masculine gender-identity in early childhood. This theory is based on the premise that the primary caretaker of an infant has virtually always been a women or women. In this situation the only rounded model of gender-identity available to the child is the feminine model displayed by the female caretaker or caretakers. The more erratic presence of males does not allow the boy to develop a positive, rounded model of masculine gender-identity. Boys learn to establish a masculine identity by negative methods, that is, by seeking to behave in ways which prove that they are not females. This comprises behaviour which deliberately avoids open display of caring, nurturing and other characteristics associated with being 'feminine'. The problematic nature of establishing masculine identity also produces the need to establish the value of masculinity by defining some activities as exclusively masculine, forbidden to females and often as beyond the capacity of the latter. Easlea sees the search by patriarchal males for this elusive masculinity as the root of their search for power over other men, over women and over nature.

Examples can be multiplied. Another case in point is the way establishment history has been written. The questions it asks and the areas of human experience it sees as having historical significance virtually confine its attention to male experience, and to that of a tiny fraction of males at that. A similar pattern recurs across the board in the knowledge and theory validated as the 'mainstream' in discipline after discipline.

Feminist criticism, then, has seen, named and defined the patriarchy that pervades our western intellectual inheritance. It has revealed the patterns of explicit denigration, objectification and subordination of women in the world-view of many of the 'master' minds of that culture. It has uncovered the hidden patriarchal framework within which much apparently neutral

5. Nancy Chodorow, *The reproduction of mothering: psychoanalysis and the sociology of gender,* California U.P. 1978. Dorothy Dinnerstein, in *The rocking of the cradle and the ruling of the world,* Souverin Press, London 1978, also explains the origins of patriarchy as rooted in the problematic establishing of male gender-identity in societies where early child-care is female dominated.

and gender-free knowledge has been constructed. It has shown how patriarchal value-systems can lead to patriarchal methodologies in scientific inquiry. It has pointed to their potential to lead to internally contradictory lines of reasoning and down socially dangerous intellectual avenues.

In doing this it establishes that sexism in education does not stop with discriminatory attitudes about who learns what and why. The expression 'boys' subjects' takes on an added meaning related to actual content. This has implications for feminist strategies. We can use positive discrimination and encouragement to build girls' confidence. We can produce non-sexist textbooks. But we cannot rewrite Aristotle, Aquinas, the development of modern science and the rest. Patriarchal values are so deeply embedded in our culture that it is simply not possible that females and males can share a similar experience in their encounter with it.

Does it follow that the problem of eliminating sexism in education is intractable? Is patriarchal thinking so pervasive and long-lived that it will never be possible to erradicate it? The revelation of the pervasiveness of patriarchy in our culture certainly establishes that the problem is bigger than many of us may have realised. Not only is it bigger but there is no question of neutralising or erasing it. The existence and the extent of patriarchy has to be recognised and accepted. Paradoxically, recognition and acceptance may point the way to another strategy. As patriarchy is forced out of the shadows onto the centre stage strange things begin to happen. Under the spotlight of feminist scrutiny one of patriarchy's most striking characteristics is seen to be its ability to avoid detection and remain effectively invisible.

Obviously it is not invisible in any literal sense. Aristotle and many of the other patriarchal thinkers were only too explicit in the articulation of their views about women. Yet generation after generation of women and men have gone through the formal and informal educational systems of western societies without ever becoming aware of the patriarchal value-system within which so much of what they learn has been constructed. It would be more accurate to say without ever coming to know it as a named and definable paradigm. This distinction between levels of awareness needs to be examined. It carries serious

6. Jean-Jacques Rousseau, *Émile*, (1765), Dent, London 1974, Introduction by P. D. Jimack.

implications for how we all, women and men, know ourselves and locate ourselves within our culture.

Lynda Lange, in her discussion of Aristotle, points to some of the methods by which patriarchy succeeds in avoiding detection or, if detected, in avoiding analysis. She notes how modern scholars regularly treat instances of patriarchy as isolated occurances and not as part of a pattern. This allows them to treat the instances as aberrations or as irrelevant to the 'main' body of thought in question, and so they avoid discussing them seriously.

A recent edition of Rousseau's *Émile* demonstrates this strategy in action and shows how explicit patriarchy can virtually disappear from sight if it is trivialised. *Émile* is, among other things, an exposition of Rousseau's blueprint for the ideal education. One of its most striking aspects is the contrast between his view as to the purpose of a boy's education and the purpose of a girl's education. The education of a boy proceeds by carefully planned stages to culminate in the emergence of an autonomous adult human being, capable of making his own responsible moral judgments. The education of a girl is explicitly designed to achieve an objective the exact reverse of this. Rousseau explains that woman's function in society is to serve man's needs and comforts. Therefore her education must be 'relative' to his. He explains at length how she must be systematically trained to subordination and service and deliberately taught to suppress the exercise of independent judgment in favour of blind acceptance of the authority and beliefs of parents and husband. For Rousseau the education of women was an important part of his philosophy of education and he develops his ideas at length. However, the twenty-six page introduction to this edition dismisses the question of women's education in six lines with the comment that Rousseau was as retrograde on this subject as he was enlightened regarding men's education and that 'Sophie will be little more than a charming plaything for Émile'.[7]

While appearing to disassociate itself from Rousseau's sexism this sort of treatment in fact compounds it and is itself sexist in a more invidious way. Rousseau himself considered the education of women to be an important issue and devoted a good deal of space to it. But the mesage from this introduction

7. *Ibid.*, p xviii.

is that it does not really matter that Rousseau held these views and that they are not worth considering as we get down to the important issue which is his discussion of men's education. If the relegation of half the human race to a state of perpetual childhood and dependence is not seen as an important part of a philosopher's system of thought the reason can only be that — at least in the eyes of those who are doing the seeing — the female half of the race is not as important (or not as fully human?) as the male half. And, of course, that is exactly how patriarchy sees it.

Another regularly encountered strategy which avoids confronting the reality of patriarchy is the argument that it is somehow unfair or invalid to draw attention to the patriarchal values in the system of ideas of a particular philosopher *because* the individual in question was merely reflecting the accepted consensus of his period. This argument shows how genuinely invisible sexism can be to people socialised within a patriarchal society. It uses the real problem, which is that a patriarchal value-system *was* the dominant paradigm in a society, as an excuse for not examining individual arguments for institutionalised sexism.

Until something is named and defined it is impossible to think about it in an ordered way, still less to discuss it. Our cultural and intellectual inheritance is presented to us as a distillation and synthesis of the highest human achievement, and as universal and gender-free. This increases the power of its underlying patriarchy to mould our self images. Patriarchy itself is not presented to us as an explicit world-view susceptible to challenge and possible rebuttal. Instead it is something we became aware of gradually, and then as something taken for granted by everyone else, too obvious and universal to require any comment. Since it is neither named nor defined there has been no accepted vocabulary available to girls and women who become uneasily aware of their status as outsider in the perspective of the 'I' of western culture.

I have a vivid personal recollection of the anxiety and insecurity about one's identity that this can lead to. Somewhere around the age of nine or ten it began to be forced on my consciousness that there was a basic incompatibility between my perception of myself and the perception of females in the world of literature I was at the time exploring. I had always identified with the active 'I' who saw, had ideas, made decisions, acted on

145

her own initiative, and could take leadership roles. I now became aware that the culture I belonged to defined this type of identity as masculine and the preserve of males. Its definition of a feminine identity, to which as a female I seemed relegated, was alien to my perception of myself. I did not experience myself as by nature passive, dependent on the leadership of others, the one who stayed at home to wait and to provide service, and I found this definition of being a female both alien and diminishing.

My encounter with the patriarchal stereotypes came in the form of a gradually developing belief that these were taken for granted by the world in general as true, universal and eternal. I had never heard of patriarchy or stereotypes. I literally had no words with which to define or think through the trauma. The only conclusion appeared to be that I was somehow peculiar and different to all other females who never questioned this situation. Even the occasional one who did for a while, like Jo in *Little Women,* eventually accepted 'femininity' to general applause. It did not occur to me that to other females I did not appear to question the stereotypes either.

The result was years of ambivalence and inhibition, sporadic efforts at conformity to the stereotype, guilt because of failure, and an eventual rejection of the stereotype as too damaging to me as a person to be tolerated any longer. Even this was a purely personal decision and involved no serious questioning of the general validity of the stereotype. That came later when I had discovered feminism.

Patriarchy, then, adopts a number of stratagems to escape detection. Its basic ploy is to maintain a low profile and so hope to pass unnoticed. When caught in the act, so to speak, it resorts to various excuses and alibis. Isolated instances may be explained as untypical aberrations. A paradigm may claim to be no more than a 'traditional' value-system that has long since ceased to be taken seriously. A contradictory stratagem, the one I encountered as a child, is to represent itself as a 'natural' and eternal set of values that are so rooted in human nature that there is no point in rebelling against them. These contradictions also slip by unnoticed in the general successful avoidance of investigation. This ability of patriarchy to make itself effectively invisible constitutes a major survival technique by maximising its power and minimising the possibility of challenge and rebuttal.

While patriarchy remains invisible and unrecognised each succeeding generation is cut off from awareness of one of the major influences which have moulded women's and men's perceptions of themselves as individual human beings located at a particular place and time in the history of western culture. Patriarchal values have influenced our lives in fundamental ways. The invisibility of these values has meant that in each generation only a small minority of women — and a much smaller minority of men— have painfully struggled through to a recognition and an analysis of this influence. By the time most of that small minority achieve this they are well into adulthood. Adjustments, changes of direction, renegotiation of sex roles, all of these are difficult and often fraught with pain for oneself and for others. The time and energy expended in what is essentially a struggle to get back to the original starting point could have been used to push forward the search for the limits of individual potential.

For the others, the majority, the starting point is never regained and they are correspondingly diminished in that they never come to a realisation of the power exerted over them by the patriarchal value-system. Its defences are too strong. It is, of course, part of this value-system to believe that what is important, significant and all-embracingly 'human' comes from the male-centred 'mainstream', and that women's experience and women-centred values are somehow outside this, in the margin or the footnote, and never an integral and essential part of mainstream human experience. The general popular response to feminist criticism and theory is that, at best, it exaggerates and magnifies the oppression of women, and, at worst, misinterprets as oppression what is in reality natural and in the best interests of both women and men.

Making the patriarchy in our culture visible is arguably one of the most important challenges facing feminism. It may well prove to be one of the most difficult. Difficult or not it appears vital for the success of strategies aimed at the elimination of sexism in education that the patriarchy that permeates our intellectual inheritance itself becomes part of the curriculum studied in the educational system, to be named, defined and analysed like any other component.

Making patriarchy visible to everyone from the time they begin to learn about their world would break the circle of a continuous reinvention of the wheel in generation after generation. If we can get the current reinvention to stick and to become part of the mainstream we will have achieved a fundamental step forward in the unfinished feminist revolution in education. The first stage is to aim for a situation in which writers of textbooks and teachers in schools and universities explicitly teach students to recognise and name patriarchal language, attitudes and paradigms wherever they meet them.

With the tools of identification and naming would come the power and freedom to consider the claims of patriarchy on its intrinsic merits as a value-system created by human minds and not as either a quaint and now out-dated curiosity or an eternal verity rooted in human nature. Once recognised and named patriarchal values can be confronted and challenged. It is easier to argue with the concrete assertions of an Aristotle or a Rousseau once these are identified as patriarchal, accepted as important and separated from a mystique which suggests that they are part of some vague but universal and infallible reality which transcends any internal irrationalies or other flaws we may detect. Teaching patriarchy as part of the curriculum creates this situation. It provides the vocabulary, the context and the permission to examine the merits of patriarchy for ourselves and to argue back and reject it if we so choose. Visibility breaks the strength patriarchy derives from its present invisibility.

This stage has been reached by a series of steps. The first was to demonstrate that patriarachy was so embedded in the body of knowledge and theory passed on as the western intellectual inheritance that in every encounter with the latter we are faced by a world view that reinforces the patriarchal stereotypes. Then it was argued that this world-view gains added power by virtue of the fact that it manages to avoid identification and challenge. The next step was to argue that, if patriarchy was to be effectively challenged, it had to be made visible.

Making patriarchy visible will cut it down to size in other ways as well. More is involved in the revolution in education than giving individuals the tools and authority to challenge patriarchal values. Visibility would also lead to fundamental changes in the composition of the body of knowledge and theory taught in the different areas. Individual instances of patriarchy could no longer escape serious examination by passing themselves off as isolated aberrations untypical of an essentially non-sexist culture. Once they were taken seriously one result would be that feminist challenges to patriarchy could no longer be ignored or excluded as irrelevant to the important issues. Mary Wollstonecraft's *A vindication of the rights of woman*[8] is an obvious case in point. Once it is accepted that the patriarchy in *Émile* is an integral part of Rousseau's system of ideas, then Wollstonecraft's vigorously argued refutation of that patriarchy takes its place as part of the eighteenth-century Enlightenment debate about education. Wollstonecraft tackled the central issue of the double standard regarding the purpose of education and put it bluntly. Either men accepted that women were rational creatures as men were and both sexes were educated to a responsible exercise of reason and judgment or they had to explicitly state that they did not believe women were rational creatures in the way men were.

The process would be repeated in discipline after discipline. For example, mainstream history would have to recognise the legal, economic and social position of women at specific places and periods as a legitimate and integral part of that mainstream. It would have to similarly recognise the organised feminist movements which challenged and changed that position. Inevitably this would involve more than a simple process of adding on new information to the existing body. Major readjustments and reassessments of current judgments, rankings and periodisation would certainly follow.

As the dust settled after these upheavals it would be found that the landscape had altered irreversibly. Patriarchal knowledge does not in reality constitute our entire cultural inheritance. It has appeared to because the selection and validation of the essential synthesis or core of human achievement has been done by dominant establishments working within a patriarchal paradigm. Feminist dissent and women-centred knowledge has been systematically excluded. This does not necessarily imply a deliberate conspiracy. Within the terms of reference of patriarchy the important mainstream *can* only be patriarchal knowledge and feminist dissent and women-centred knowledge are eternally peripheral.

Feminist scholars have made considerable progress in the re-discovery of this other inheritance. Much may have been lost for ever but it is already clear that a considerable amount has only been 'mislaid'. Indeed, given that patriarchal establish-

8. Mary Wollstonecraft, *A vindication of the rights of women,* (1792).

ments seldom actively encouraged or fostered feminist challenges to themselves, and still less facilitated their publication and dissemination, the present state of the art indicates that an impressive amount surmounted the obstacles and succeeded in achieving publication.[9] Given the difficulties it seems reasonable to infer that what is being rediscovered represents the tip of an iceberg. If patriarchy can be made visible — and then kept visible — the gradual assessment and incorporation of the feminist tradition into the mainstream promises to be a stimulating and exhilerating development.

Many of the questions we now ask about the relationships between women and men will change as the patriarchal paradigm loosens its hold. Women will no longer appear only as hitherto excluded outsiders now demanding access to the knowledge men have created. Patriarchal knowledge will be relegated to its proper place as knowledge created within the framework of one particular world-view, and an obviously flawed world-view at that. Apologias for women's lack of contribution will become redundant and irrelevant. Instead, patriarchal thinking will be seen to require apologias — and apologies. Its origin and development will become a priority focus for research as the evidence of the damage done to individuals of both sexes by patriarchal stereotypes is studied and as its suggested links to threats to the continued existence of the race are further explored.

Feminist perspectives also open the way to the creation of new paradigms and to the building of new knowledge and theory. Where patriarchy is a closed system which restricts development and which contains within itself no possibilities of creative growth feminism has the potential to reach out to and interact with other perspectives and paradigms to their mutual enrichment. The currently ongoing encounter between feminism and socialism is a case in point. Feminism's basic strength is that it starts from the experience of individual women who find that patriarchal stereotypes are damaging to their development as human persons. It follows that feminism is essentially concerned with definitions of what it is to be a human being and that it looks for definitions which encourage rather than limit growth. Because of this base in women's experience of patriarchal stereotypes the thrust of feminism is

9. See, for example, the work of Dale Spender.

always against the imposition of rigid definitions and enforced conformity. Its perspectives contribute to the richness and diversity of exploration of the potential of human nature for both women and men. Its contribution has already shown itself to be of major significance.

Feminist perspectives on the history of the western intellectual tradition reject the dualisms which have been such a restricting feature. Instead of the continual positing of opposites, masculinity and femininity, mind and body, rational and irrational, and the continual positing of hierarchies of power, feminism contributes to a wider and richer evaluation. 'Minds and bodies, not the mind and the body; men and women, not the male and the female; masculinities and femininities, not the masculine and the feminine; sexualities and genderisations — the plurals will come forward, and the past will be viewed as a resource, not just as a tragedy'.[10]

Making what is already there visible sounds a straightforward and relatively simple undertaking. It is optimistic to think that it will turn out to be so. We need not expect that any stage in the unfinished revolution in education will be easy. It is true that the basis for the next stage already exists in the growing body of feminist knowledge, theory and criticism. But drawing on it to revolutionise the way in which the cultural inheritance is passed on either within or without the formal educational system will not be easily achieved. Entrenched patriarchal value-systems militate against taking feminist scholarship seriously just as they militate against seeing or discussing patriarchy itself. However, we can take courage from the historical record which shows that feminist dissent and the creation and expression of feminist knowledge and theory has never been fully suppressed even when it has been excluded from the body of knowledge and theory validated and approved by dominant patriarchal establishments. The knowledge that this is so can give courage and hope to those who believe that the contribution of feminist scholarship is an essential step towards the education of both sexes to their full human potential.

10.   Elisabeth Young-Bruehl, 'The education of women as philosophers', in *Signs,* vol. 12, no. 2, winter 1987, p. 214.